Poetry Ireland Review 125

Eagarthóir / Editor
EAVAN BOLAND

Poetry Ireland Ltd/Éigse Éireann Teo gratefully acknowledges the assistance of The Arts Council/An Chomhairle Ealaíon and The Arts Council of Northern Ireland.

Poetry Ireland invites individuals and commercial organizations to become Friends of Poetry Ireland. For more details, please contact: Poetry Ireland Friends Scheme, Poetry Ireland, 11 Parnell Square East, Dublin 1, Ireland or telephone +353 1 6789815; e-mail info@poetryireland.ie

FOUNDING PARTNERS
Adrian Brinkerhoff Poetry Fund of the Sidney E Frank Foundation

POETRY PATRONS: EPIC
Thomas Dillon Redshaw

POETRY PATRONS: LYRIC
Eithne Hand, Ruth Webster

POETRY PATRONS: SONNET
Anonymous, Neville Keery, Nana Lampton, William McConkey, Joan and Joe McBreen

POETRY PATRON: HAIKU
Ciara McCluskey

FRIENDS OF POETRY IRELAND
Desmond Windle, Rachel Joynt, Noel and Anne Monahan, Maurice Earls, Mary Shine Thompson, Seán Coyle, Andrew Caldicott, Henry and Deirdre Comerford

ISBN: 978-1-902121-72-7
ISSN: 0332-2998

PUBLICATIONS MANAGER: Paul Lenehan, with the assistance of Bailey Kendall, Chase Wilmot, and Moira Cardiff
IRISH-LANGUAGE EDITOR: Caitlín Nic Íomhair
DESIGN: Alistair Keady (www.hexhibit.com)
COVER CREDIT: *Out of the Shadows* (2017) by Will St Leger

Contents   POETRY IRELAND REVIEW 125

Editorial

In September of last year, Poetry Ireland hosted a focus group of poets, activists, critics, students, and teachers to discuss diversity. The Poetry Ireland team ably co-ordinated an event with many voices and differing perspectives. Earlier in the year, in May 2017, Poetry Ireland had re-stated its commitment to promote the 'best practice models on diversity and gender balance across all areas of our work'. The focus group was one outcome of this commitment. I was present with others at the discussion in September, as was the American poet Kevin Young. The conversation that day mirrored some of the concerns of the West coast in the US where I work. The issues raised are central now to poetry everywhere. They are issues of inclusion and permission. They already affect many of the emerging poets this journal publishes. So it seems worthwhile to register some of the arguments here.

The conversation in September was informative. The details were often surprising and compelling, and the conversation often eloquent and moving. Poets in the room with an awareness of ethnicity, of gender, of disability, of sexual difference, voiced their sense that their poetry spoke from and should record these realities; poets who valued performance and others who relied on the page spoke about this; poets who led urban workshops and some who fostered online communications described their different knowledges. They advocated for these experiences not only because they formed their identities, but because those identities were forming a richer sense of the poems they wrote.

I was a listener there. Many of the details I didn't know and wouldn't presume to comment on. But if I didn't know the occasion, I certainly knew the conversation. I have known it for a long time. There is no more difficult and no more important ongoing discussion in the arts. Yet anyone who knows the poetry world knows how powerful is the resistance to this conversation about diversity. Many of the holders of conservative opinions see themselves as gate-keepers and hold positions of influence and access: publishers, editors, prize committee members. They are able to resist change under the banner of standards and to marginalize dissent with the argument that these energies amount to little but social engineering. For many emerging poets – poets of colour, of gender diversity, of sexual difference, of aesthetic dissent – this resistance can be daunting.

Diversity in poetry is interpreted by sceptics as being merely about social change. In reality, it is about formal and artistic renewal. Anyone reading twentieth century poetry from Allen Ginsberg to Adrienne Rich to Medbh McGuckian has to know that the margin re-defines the centre, and not the other way around. But that margin has to be visible, has to be vocal, has to be sustained by new critiques as well as new poems. If not, poetry will be held hostage to outdated critiques in which are coded old resistances. For that reason, diversity has to be recognised and supported. When I was younger, the coded critiques suggesting that the expressive lives of women would distort the Irish poem seemed to me wrong then. And wrong now. The contemporary codes today inferring that diversity is a social project not a poetic one seem equally wrong.

We need to emphasise the importance of diversity not simply because it's about the future of society, but because it points to the future of poetry. The old conservative mantra that self-expression is not art leaves a question hanging. Who is to arbitrate that difference? Who is to say when one becomes the other? Without a generous vital conversation about diversity, such as Poetry Ireland is undertaking, the question will remain stalled, mired in divisive and limiting arguments.

Despite my own disagreements with purists in the profession over many years, I've often recognised their sincerity, their love for the craft, their deep frustration with what they see as the blurring of lines separating an old art from a contemporary society. But the past is a safe place; the future a far more unsettled one. For all the present distrust that certainly exists, I hope that the future in poetry will be a shared one where division becomes debate, and a living speech – open to change – helps to change poetry.

– Eavan Boland

Rosamund Taylor

PRIDE 2017

Summer solstice,
we lie without covers,
room scented by buddleia.

Our new rings gleam.
This is old as kissing –
two bodies of the same kind

loving one another. We are new
because promises we made bind us
in law as well as love.

At the close of the Soviet Union,
we were born: you on the Polish border,
I by Scotsman's Bay.

We didn't know it was the right time –
strangers already marched for us.
In bitter years of boys' hands up our shirts,

our names on bus stops and walls,
we didn't know our luck:
that we would find this moment

when we sleep safe
this shortest night,
and wake to a rainstorm,

frogs leaping in yarrow and lady's bedstraw.

Knute Skinner

THE RASPBERRY TARTS

We had lots of good food for Dottie's tenth birthday party.
Gertie made her renowned potato salad
while I sliced platefuls of pumpernickel, ham and cheese.
To top it all off we had pumpkin – Dottie's favourite ice cream –
as well as Gertie's raspberry tarts.

Her tarts, you could say, were as famous
as was her potato salad.
She took great pains with each tart
and always made just enough.

"Two apiece would be trouble," she always said,
and whatever she meant by that I never knew.

Well, the party did start off all right,
but then who should show up but the Koppermann twins?
Their mother had told me expressly that they couldn't make it.

But make it they did, and what could we do about it?
I offered to go without my tart, but Gertie –
well Gertie stubbornly said she would not.
(Gertie was already turning a bit funny).

Well, in the end I asked Dottie to do without hers –
a fine thing was *that* on her birthday.

*

That party was, of course, a long time ago,
just two years before Gertie packed it all up
in a jabbering fit on the way to Emergency.

Dottie? Oh, she's away on the Florida coast.
I hear from her now and then
and always at Christmas.

She tells me she has a job working for tourists,
but I've heard rumours.

Moya Cannon

BREAD

The suitcase is only half-unpacked
the washing not done,
the floor not swept,
but the oven is humming,
a sticky bowl and spoon
are in the sink
and the old alchemy of water,
flour and leaven has begun.

Soon the high crusts will gild,
three loaves will be tapped
from their tins,
an aroma will flow
through keyholes;
will slip over chipped saddleboards,

proclaiming more eloquently
than a thrush delivering
its blue and gold aria
from the top of a telegraph pole,
than a procession
with lifted banners
and trumpets,
than a dog panting wagging circles
around a kitchen,
Home, home, home, home, home.

Derek Mahon

OPHELIA

It started at nine in the morning as things do.
The eye of the cyclone remained out at sea
but we got the hard edge as it hit the coast
and, anti-clockwise, strove to devastate
a province; the lights failed and slates flew
while I sat it out here in 'excited reverie'
listening to climate change doing its work
with a stereophonic front of punitive rain.
Too much of water, fierce 'Ophelia', when
sea overwhelms our shaky earthworks. (Who
names storms, who names the winds and stars?)
No birds sing in this ominous half-dark.
We wait for daylight in the daylight hours
and, reading by candlelight as in other ages,
picture the whirling vortex, the wave surges
storming ashore; the roaring blitz of it.
It must be a sign of something, but of what?
The death of world civilization, I suppose,
and man-made climate is the evident cause –
which raises the grim question of what next?

   Now lights come on and the fridge shakes,
the phone speaks in a tone of huge relief;
whatever was under wraps returns to life.
Everything picks up with the sky at rest
and nothing to scare us for a while at least.
A bit like Key West in the strange aftermath,
whipping and dripping, the storm took a path
due north and died at last over Donegal,
just a high whistling wind like any gale,
nothing remarkable. Maybe Ophelia too
was nothing special, merely first of a new
series of weather events to be lived through.
Cyclones, of course, shouldn't come up this far
into our mild, predictable temperate zone
but rage down there below the blue horizon
like fire and pestilence; yet here they are,
one further import from the Angrian shore.
   Ophelia, royal girlfriend not the wind,
withdrew to nature like a sensible maid

but chose a flowing stream and willow shade –
a dubious option, not the best of choices,
and one she'd have refused in her right mind;
but it does get harder by the year to find
sanctuary from the clamour of crazed voices.
So shut the hatches, fill the shelves and hoard
candles against the dark time coming on
when hubris reaches for the infinite spaces
in a true cyclone spun by fatal industries
with this one filed as just an autumn breeze,
one of many before the real thing began.

Derek Mahon

TRUMP TIME

1

Nineveh, Tyre and Carthage are long gone;
also Troy and the hanging gardens of Babylon.
Now Britain's empire is a thing of the past
and Angria too will have an end at last –
oh, not an end, but a slow decline at least.
Whitman and *Moby-Dick*, F. Scott Fitzgerald
will still be read, Gershwin and Satchmo heard,
movies downloaded; but the wider world
will think of other things, as it did once.
Hard rock and carpet bombing will be down,
Apple and Goldman Sachs down with the rest,
some peace and quiet once again in evidence.

2

Where a spring rises, in the little wood
of birch and sycamore beside the house,
I stand and listen to the undying source
whispering there. I'd travel if I could
through the lost ages to a distant time
when it was sacred to a pre-Christian god;
I'd tie a token on a thorn and climb
back to the present, sure in the belief
we can still touch the origins of life,
relish perspective, silence, solitude
far from the bedlam of acquisitive force
that rules us and would rule the universe.

3

Such things survive, beloved of poet and artist,
only where their despoilers haven't noticed –
in a yard or a hidden cove, out on the edge,
the rushy meadow and the fallow acre
ripe for development as industrial plant.
Serving as temple, shrine and sepulchre,
these places minister to the soul by dint
of radiating a strange air of privilege;
and here we live, not in a petulant rage
for world dominion but an inner continent
of long twilights shrouded in mist and rain,
the lasting features of our lost domain.

Partridge Boswell

ODE TO INVASIVE SPECIES

You'll need a cement jaw, gloves of thick raw-
hide and bombproof canvas pants, a sharp spade
maybe a pick to pry soil loose around the base,

a mild day after a night of rain to soften their
resolve, an intolerant epithet or two to remind
them who owns the sun and rain, the nutrient-

rich loam here merely on loan. Loppers alone
won't do. You'll need to grab low, yank and
wrench maybe even dig before roots unscrew

their tapered lengths from rhizomatic recesses
lukewarm & dark as the womb of a surrogate
who consents to birth but not to motherhood.

You'll need a uniformed conservation corps
of eager unformed youth who won't connect
the green sweat of just another summer job

with an angry mob's generic objective, who
will hear in their names only the thorn in buck-
thorn, the strife in loosestrife, the knot in knot-

weed, the suck in honeysuckle, the Russian
in Russian olive, the false in false indigo, the
heave in tree of heaven. Access to a 24/7 news

channel might help, but since your genocide's
low tech, all you'll really need is the hook of
a melody's veiled invective, catchy as *Sweet*

Home Alabama where kudzu runs more rampant
than whatever genus crooned the land back to
sleep after the Centennial Exposition where

the miraculous new plant from Japan was first
introduced along with the telephone and type-
writer and their unborn progeny of devices

that are now more endemic than air.

Kerry Hardie

WARMING THE ROOM

Philip Schultz, *Luxury* (WW Norton and Co, 2018), $26.95 hb.
Carol Rumens, *Animal People* (Seren Books, 2016), £9.99.
Ian Duhig, *The Blind Road-Maker* (Picador Poetry, 2016), £9.99.

Not a book for the down-hearted, Philip Schultz's *Luxury* sees its author
a-spin in a vortex of self-examination that ends with his realisation that
the state of happiness is the ultimate luxury. The only problem I have
with this conclusion (and with the book) is the length of time / thought he
takes to reach what seems to be a fairly self-evident truth. Schultz rarely
writes a bad line, is unafraid of metaphysical speculation, and his voice
speaks throughout with admirable clarity and simplicity. The first poem,
'Paraphernalia', is as intelligent and appealing a picture of someone
trapped inside the litter of a life with which he no longer identifies, as I
have read in a long time:

> ... while my soul waits patiently
> at the door, hoping I'll remember my sunglasses,
> car keys, and Penelope, in my hurry to be obsolete.

But this is about as cheerful as it gets, for the side-lining he describes so
well rapidly gives way to a vague anxiety which seems to be the lot of
many fairly well-heeled suburban dwellers in the affluent West, who
wake one morning wondering what life is all about. Hard on this comes
the questioning. If life is as pointless as it seems to be and the world has
been hijacked 'on its way to a barricaded future / on the far side of a
fence where all our significance is buried', then what is the reason for
continuing to occupy a seat on the bus on which we are all travelling?
Despair follows hard on the always devastating realisation that the grave
is getting horribly close and precisely what have you done with your time
in the world?

Schultz's narrative gifts are considerable, and the glimpses he gives
us of his own life are finely drawn and tinged with irony or sorrow or
both. He always steers his narrative just this side of tragedy and, with
admirable self-deprecation, refuses to explore his own particular despair,
but hands it over to others (Hemingway, Celan, his friend R.). I liked this
book, but when I hit the long meditation on suicide, I did find myself
wondering why it feels a little banal. Look at these lines from 'Sadness':

Suddenly,
regardless of what the gods say,
the present remains uninhabitable,
the past unforgiving of the harm it's seen.

Surely there is no arguing with a present that is 'uninhabitable'? I think
part of the problem of this book is that Schultz's personal history contains
pain and disappointment but little tragedy, and he is too honest to pretend
otherwise. His is a fortunate life in an unfortunate world, yet one that
fails to deliver on meaning. Intelligent and self-aware, he understands this
state but can't quite seem to accept it, while knowing that he ought to.
He has lived his life with 'colourful ladies and well-bred men', has already
survived one youthful suicide attempt, and is unlikely to die 'bankrupt
and penniless' as his father before him has done. As well as all this, there
is the dream 'of a family house', and a future containing blackbirds and
deer and 'a notion / …as fragrant / and luxurious/as happiness'. This
is the rub: the dream has been realised but the happiness has proved
elusive. He is so balanced and modest in his sense of what is owed him
that he downplays his own despair and the writing rarely takes wing as
it might. Yet his conclusion is correct: the 'luxury' of happiness is a rare
thing, attained by few.

If Schultz's tone is open, even, and self-deprecating, Carol Rumens'
is hermetic. *Animal People* reminded me a bit of a rock-pool lined with
assorted crustaceans, requiring effort and dedication to prise open.
Sometimes, no matter how much I wrenched and scraped, the mollusc
refused to open. More often the result was alienating and/or disappointing, as the opened shell felt empty of anything more than a successfully
rendered poetic exercise.

But from time to time the shell opened under the knife and behind
the salt-flesh mass of the poem there gleamed the authentic sheen of
pearl. This is true of the wonderful 'From an Evening Walk-Diary', with
its luminous closing lines: 'Slow spring dusks, you remind me/of the last
lap of age, how stretched and fine the days there.'

Another such poem is 'Small Facts', with its steady refusal of any comfort, despite her enormous loss:

Fact: I shall not re-make
my snow-man beliefs,
nor think it consolation
ever that you – or any
creature in its un-making –
"quietly"   "sleeps."

Best of all was the final sequence 'On the Spectrum', which is described
on the book cover as an attempt to explore what it means to be 'on the

autistic spectrum'. This sequence is difficult to paraphrase or to understand in literal terms, yet is oddly moving and left me with the feeling of
having spent time inside a way of being that I had not previously explored.
Try this for dysfunction/disjunction/illumination:

> How does those girls know the same secret and say it
> how are their sharing without it words or why
> is the hair so bright and pale and what are they laughing?

I have rarely read a better description of a child alone and adrift in an
incomprehensible world, and after it, the mollusc-like nature of many
of the poems I had already read seemed less alienating. I found myself
re-reading them in the light of their author's sense of being 'wrongly
psyched', of her attempts 'to edit it all to all right', of her conviction that
she was using metaphors that are 'slipped rind'.

Yet for all this, I find myself writing a disappointed review: disappointed
because it is disappointing not to find more to excite in the work of a
poet as erudite and skilled as Rumens. There is no quarrelling with her
technical assurance and her ease with form and word-play, but too many
of the more open poems feel like commissions or exercises done with
or for students, and I wonder again about poets who spend too much of
their lives attached to universities.

Ian Duhig's *The Blind Road-Maker*, though a bit over-burdened with
references to Sterne and *Tristram Shandy*, is a well-crafted, clever book,
with a real feeling for the rhythms and territories of his poetic predeces-
sors. He can adopt a poet's persona, frequently in mockery of his own
('Long Will') ...

> Now I'm brought back by a fart of a bard,
> to rage and to rant in my *rum, ram, ruff* staves

... and give us essence of Langland: a strong taste in the mouth and a back
bowed from the weight of clod-heavy ploughshare language. Equally, he
can do the labyrinthine swerves and turns of Sterne, or the bawdy, clever
lines (all immaculately rhymed and metred) of a Byronesque romp.
There is a real love of music behind his love of words, and from time to
time he will use an old form (as with 'The Passion of the Holly') to strike
a sudden and genuine note of gravitas to weight the sheets of paper flying
from his printer.

> O our holly and its berry were soon turned to dust,
> as were we who in singing and kindness put trust;
> and yet though we sing now to you from the grave,
> you can hear us because we are singing of love.

Or, from 'The Year's Mind, Ripon':

> The Clock warns *'Except ye Lord keep*
> *ye Cittie ye Wakeman waketh in vain'*;
> vain the fool waking those not asleep.
> The Skell gathers itself to drown again.

So quicksilver are all these twists and turns that you sometimes catch yourself wondering if Duhig is here at all, or if he only lives through other people's stories and the way he sees them watching him at work. I did think I'd glimpsed him in 'Rum' and in 'Square Ring', but he is too clever to sit still for long and, like a man with a talent for impersonation, he quickly grows bored with his own voice and picks up someone else's. Easy enough when there is always another irresistibly weird story out there waiting to be told ('Jade Pilot'), another form waiting to be explored, a new idea to riff on. But sometimes these bravado flourishes are the nearest he comes to tripping himself up. Though clever, his appropriation of Burns's wonderful love song is essentially trite ('Bridled Vows'), and the prose poem, 'Shapeshifting Ghosts of Byland Abbey', reads like a sub-Poe fantasy.

But overall this is a fine book, marred only by too many commissioned works, which play to the strengths of the head and do not demand of the poet the discipline of waiting for the poem that 'sits and waits, / warms the room / arranges all to make it welcoming' (from 'Ghostspeaking', by Peter Boyle). Were he to turn down a few of the commissions and sit and wait for the poem that is sitting waiting, he might write an even better book.

Ethna McKiernan

STORM, LAKE SUPERIOR

If ever I were ever to fall in love
again, it's likely not
to be with someone human,
but with a moment just like this one –

a lit expanse of water during storm
forked by lightning from sky to lake,
some crazed colour between silver and white –
light flashing staccato below a grey band

of clouds, waves that bluster in
while wind billows and thunder rumbles
deep. There I'd know a hum
of both aloneness and connection,

sky brilliant and alive, stars electric
after rain, the aftermath of storm
searing through my brain
with a depth I've never known.

Martina Evans

LOVE

I couldn't help it.
I gathered cats and dogs to my chest
I love you I love you I said,
squeezing them hard
even though I knew they didn't like it.
I wanted to be gentle like Daddy – dogs' eyes swam
when he placed his crooked swollen hands on their hairy brows.
I'm back, I'm back! he shouted
as his seventeen cats poured in an unbroken pilgrimage
down the fragmented path to greet him
after any absence. They quivered
at the sound of his flat County Limerick accent
nuzzled into what he called their *vessels*
old tin lids piled up with chunks of ham, corned beef
chicken and ham roll stolen from the shop.
Feed all the birds – that was his policy,
he tossed pieces of Keating's fresh pan into the air.
Sparrow, blackbird, jackdaw, crow or pigeon,
not one bird was classified as vermin –
only the flies were a different kettle of fish.
Eschewing spray,
he favoured the quiet stickiness of fly paper:
twelve amber strips hung,
streaming from the low wood ceiling of the shop
and he moved among them like a gardener
hissing gently.

Sean H McDowell

CHICKEN SOUP

She threw away what others most relied on:
Neck bones, gizzards, bent wings and livers,
The carcass after the choice cuts were gone.
Even thigh bones and drumsticks, which neighbours bought
Fried by the bucket, never graced her pot.

And tailbones, *What good could come from a dead*
Bird's ass? She rinsed and trimmed four raw breasts
Of excess rubbery skin, covered them
With cold water and poured in salt measured
From her practiced palm. Her vegetables

Followed with like care. After peeling away
Their papery skin, she burned both
The tops and bottoms of two large onions
Until they blackened on an open flame.
Then three celery stalks (leaves intact)

And three carrots she snicked into thick rounds.
Next she coaxed the crammed pot to boiling,
Then set it simmering, slowly skimming
Off the grit and froth of muddying fat
As offensive to the true faith of broth.

By and by the boiling meat wept bubbles
Of pure gold, and golden too the essences
Leached from the rest till the burgeoning soup
Began darkening to a lager's hue,
Its smell warming the kitchen like a presence.

Outside, past the forked oaks, beyond the plain
Below her hill, the shipping cranes on Maumee Bay
Looked toylike in the distance and so did
The cargo ships bound for continents
My grandmother would never travel to.

By and by onions clarified. Carrots
Softened. Celery went limp. And meat
Sloughed off bones. She strained every solid

And morsel from the clear broth and added
Nothing but Kluski noodles, their foetal curls.

So she ladled her every ambition
Into the anonymity of the shallow bowl
She offered me. And so I slurped each spoonful
In disbelief that anything this precious
Could be mine for as long as it lasted.

Eleni Cay

ORANGES ARE THE ONLY FRUIT

My grandfather unwrapped his first orange when he was nine.
He didn't wash his hands till Three Kings' Day,
the sweet essence lingering on his calluses.
He used to say grandma's hugs were like oranges in winter.

My parents plundered a few when they were young.
The bold sweetness of Valencias ignited a land
of opportunity inside their mouths. They gobbled the
flesh together with the skin, blinded by the flushed sun.

Mr McPhee bought as many as the words he wrote for *The New Yorker.*
Unsure whether to cut them into nine like planets or into quarters
like lunch for the businessmen. They tasted of a pre-dawn running,
pesticide-rich, fruitless manufactured concentrate to him.

I have experienced many. Too many for one person to carry.
I calorie-checked, Instagrammed, changed them beyond recognition.
With yellow nails you carved out the seeds, *now the oranges are mine,*
you said. *No one can put fruit back together once it is cut in half.*

EE Jones

PHOENIX PARK MURDERS

06.05.1882

Another day in the archive of missed chances
Where history is folded and at peace.
Suddenly, a paper slips from my grasp
And floats to the floor: the weightlessness of the past!

I bend to retrieve a telegram that speaks
Of double murder in the park: pause
To consider how two corpses
Tipped the scales towards revenge,
The hatred on which history depends;
Then file it away between recriminations,
Nation is speaking to nation.

There was a boy on a bicycle that day
Whose great-grandchildren still leave flowers
On the path, each year, on the sixth of May,
In memory of a sunny day gone wrong:
A child's shock, his sudden strong dismay
To find two bodies bleeding on the grass –
Two casualties of a half-forgotten war
Whose public deaths mean nothing any more.

Nessa O'Mahony

LEGENDARY WOMEN, UNLEGENDARY LANDS

Rosemarie Rowley, *Girls of the Globe* (Arlen House, 2015), €13.
Rosemarie Rowley, *Ireland's Legendary Women* (Arlen House, 2016), €13.
Mary Turley-McGrath, *Other Routes* (Arlen House, 2016), €13.

There has been much discussion of late of the need to reclaim into the canon neglected women writers of the past. Reading Rosemarie Rowley's two most recent collections reminds us that not all neglected writers are in the past; we have many contemporary examples who have been plough-ing their lonely fields for many decades, and whose presence registers not even a blip on the radar of contemporary curators. Rosemarie Rowley's first collection was published in 1985; her seventh and eighth were pub-lished by Arlen House in 2015 and 2016 to scant notice, it must be said. The fact that this is only Rowley's second review in *Poetry Ireland Review* says much about the critical attention she has received. But I don't intend to spend the remainder of this space considering why her poetry hasn't been discussed, rather to give a sense of the work she does and the way she does it.

Girls of the Globe contains 84 poems, including 71 sonnets and a selection of other strictly formal poems that explore a world where the woman's voice is often silenced. The opening sequence of sonnets brings us a range of Shakespearean heroines, many of whom, like Perdita from *A Winter's Tale*, are destined to disappear until they are rescued by art: 'Yet only art can rescue the act of stealth / By which you became exile, like a tree / Turned from a god's pursuit of wealth'; or Ophelia, whose watery grave echoes Cleopatra 'freighted in gold, in a splendid barque / In which to log her passion and her pledge'. Each sonnet is beautifully turned, their Shakespearean echoes blended with a more urbane contemporary edge that brings in allusions to Lady Gaga and race relations. There are occasional poems that resist the reader's comprehension; the careful rhyme scheme locking up clarity, rather than releasing it (for example the poem 'All This Doing Good Is Very Catholic'), but mostly the rhymes and meaning work well together. The rhyme scheme of a poem such as 'Days of Reckoning' gives extra propulsion to the anger at the exploitation of a world where:

> We became mendacious
> Dealt when the god was down and out
> Gave libertine professors a lot of clout
> Gave people a push with their crime

Gave them conditions to develop
Their needy greedy ways to lop
All the leaves from the tree
As they die from the top
Of the world, all the bees
Wiped out with disease
All the putrid mannerisms
Of selfish dyed-in-the-wool schisms

In many poems, particularly those that depend on rhyming couplets, we sense the ghost of Byron's elegant political squibs, so it's not surprising to discover towards the end of this collection a longer poem, in sections, entitled 'An Overdue Letter to Lord Byron', in which she explores that debt as well as the discovery of a family connection – Rowley's ancestor fought alongside Byron's grandfather at the Battle of Grenada, in 1779. One wonders whether she is considering her own work's reception as much as his when she writes in section 7:

Some say such work is just a crafty drivel
While others moan about its bad prolixity
Still others indicate a haughty swivel
From the chairman who applauds its swift dexterity

But it's clear she doesn't regret his influence, concluding that the poet's 'magniloquence that's hardly terse, / Your mighty opus is our universe'.

In the next volume, Rowley turns her attention to the famous women of Irish myth and legend, and tells their stories in a series of heptastich (seven-line stanzas that are iambic and with rhyme scheme based on variations of *ababbcc*). The decision to give a page to each heptastich means there's quite a lot of white space, and the volume is considerably thicker than it might have been, but the other impact is that the narrative seems to move swiftly forward as these familiar tales are retold with lyrical precision. Rowley doesn't seem particularly interested in revision here – the telling seems fairly faithful to the original accounts. Here, for example, is a section from the first poem, 'The Wooing of Étain':

The High King thought she was his to woo.
And won her after a summer's night
her heart did not stir for him, as he who
rode in the memory like a vision of the light

Alongside the story of Étain, *Ireland's Legendary Women* includes the tales of Eimear, Deirdre, and Gráinne, as well as renderings of famous subjects of bardic poetry, such as O'Rahilly's 'fairest of the fair' or Kitty Dwyer, one of the endless personifications of Ireland found in the tradition. She concludes the book with her take on another iconic female subject, the grieving mother of Christ, in her poem 'The Lament of the Three Marys'. This final section is titled 'The Mother', which conjures up memories of Pearse's famous poem of the same name, but there's none of his mock-heroic victimhood in this poem; Rowley's mother grieves flesh and bone, not legendary martyr: 'Is that the infant son I bore for three seasons?' she asks, reminding us that beneath every legend there is human fact, human feeling.

A human fascination with place infuses the poetry of Donegal-based poet, Mary Turley-McGrath. In *Other Routes* she explores the 'Here' of her native and adopted landscape along with the 'There' of other territories, from Brighton's seafront to the contested locations of the Holy Land. *Dinnseanchas*, the age-old lore of place and placename, is central to her method. Many of the poems trace the seed and breed of the men and women who've walked the territory, built the walls and buildings. Even the source of the stone they used is known, as in 'The Bell Arch Date':

> One of the strong men who shaped
> stone for the twelve-foot orchard wall
> from blocks blasted in Tibarney quarry,
> then carted over the village bridge
> and up the avenue to Thornfield House.

The big house is part of that shared fabric (the eponymous 'Mount Talbot House' 'stole my soul: / drew me into its crumbling walls / through black-eyed windows'), but the natural world of beaches and headlands more frequently draws the eye: Donegal landscape is hard to ignore, after all. Turley-McGrath doesn't strive for ornateness of language; she captures the scene with a documentary, almost cinematic, sweep for detail that occasionally takes a lyric turn. In 'Magheroarty Beach' we are shown two boats lying 'under blue plastic near the pier':

> high above them the masthead wires vibrate.
> The ensign cable rings along the hollow mast,
> earthing the sound like bells at a holy place.

There's no place for myth in such a place, 'no golden girl / on a white stallion sweeping her hero to Tír na nÓg'; Turley-McGrath prefers the realism of 'two figures' that 'move towards a jeep at the sand's end', although such realism can sometimes lead to flatness of diction, as in the poem 'Winter in Donegal', where on Rathmullen Beach 'the tide was so far out / I felt it could never return'. This feels more like conversation than distilled poetic language. But elsewhere (on another beach) she can strike a more numinous note, asking, in the poem 'From the Sands':

> Was it dark matter made visible,
> that unknown part of the Universe
> revealed; or that part of ourselves
> we do not know ...

The later poems range further afield, but Turley-McGrath brings her observant eye with her wherever she travels. The poem 'In Rota' is full of evocative detail ...

> In Plaza de San Roque strollers gather
> round the chestnut seller. Steam pours
> from a tall black pipe as the nuts roast.
> Families share them from paper-twists
> and saunter by the Chapel of Vera Cruz
> where God rests under Baroque ceilings.

... whilst her Holy Land poems capture very well a place 'that cannot / make up its mind between old and new' ('First Night in Tel Aviv'). Turley-McGrath may not make us see the world in a new way, perhaps, but she reminds us constantly of what our busy eyes might overlook.

Joyce Wilson

I FREED A DOVE TODAY

Confused, she spent the night inside our shed.
Perched on a barrel rim and teetering,
She flapped to see me there, my entering
A sight that must have filled her heart with dread.
Not trusting my extended pair of hands,
She flew up to the windowpane and clung
Against the image of the world she'd sung
About before, its pleasures and demands.
The scene beyond the window stayed in view.
I improvised a perch of pole and head
Without its stringy mop, and then, with daft
Finesse, I held it up. She stepped, I led.
She saw that she could ride on this lone shaft –
And there it was! The World! And there she flew!

John Kinsella

THIS IS NO HOMESTEADER FANTASY

This is no homesteader fantasy
This is no prepper textual bunker
This is no survivalist sell for the sake of a vicarious social media following
This is no hopping-off point for the post-apocalyptic *newworld*
This is no 'wilderness' constructed by Euro-fantasists
This is no white-values enclave
This is no isolationism
This is no arsenal; no bow-hunter's arrow in the heart of the goat epiphany
This is no threat to the living or the dead
This is no blooding
This is no body-worship state-of-nature retreat into reading literature
   of the *self* trope
This is no *Thus Spake Zarathustra*
This is no inheritance of state-approved property rights
This is no getting back to transplanted ancestral roots – but this *is* a place
   of other people's ancestors who know the tricks of displacement and won't be
   shunted out by reconstructions made from paleo visions – respect *them*
This is no *children of nature* living out their middleclass exclusionism scenario
This is no 'getting away from it all' for the sake of writing-a-book-about
   The Experience for a generally white middleclass audience, with the aim
   being to move on to the next Experience and write another exposé
   ad infinitum
This is no 'off-the-grid' so we can show 'how close to nature we are and you're not'
   manifesto
This is no acceptance of the grid
This is no *becoming one* with the oppressed animals that make ends meet
   in the grinding down of bushland to a few patches which are then burnt
This is no rejection of those oppressed animals
This is nothing more than a statement of hope – a hope of minimising the damage,
   of keeping the door open to those in need, to respecting the fact (glorious fact)
   that non-human life lives here too, and has rights, if you open your
   sensibilities.

Peggie Gallagher

THE VIOLIN
after a line by Michael Longley

Stained with blood from a hare,
long-since written

into the ripple of the grain.
Listen to the slow rasp of the bow

how it searches out
that walled-up bawl of grief,

picks the lock
and slides in like a thief.

It can strike anywhere;
in a strange land

a crowded room,
a dark auditorium

salt-scald, feral
gravid as a mountain stream.

John Wall Barger

IDIOTIC RACIST BULLY SONG

The schoolkids in bright
uniforms ran down
the steps to the street.
One stopped to stare at me.
I knew him: Fang II,
son of a Chinese kid
I'd bullied in grade school,
thirty years ago. I'd sit
on his chest & ask,
"What's wong Wong?
Something wong Wong?"
He hanged himself
last year, I read. Fang II
hopped up to me like a bird,
overbite, smiling.
The basketball he held
was so clean it couldn't ever
have touched the ground.
He looked me over.
"If your body *ith* not heal*th*y,"
he lisped, "your *th*oul
can overcome it." I grinned.
"Is my body unhealthy?"
"In *th'* name of Allah, ye*th*."
I laughed in his face.
"What is *Allah*, Fang II?"
He gestured to the glass
buildings around us:
"If the*th* mountains had eye*th*,
*th*ey would be Allah*th* face."
"What does your Allah
say about *loss*, kid?"
As I said this, I rolled his ball
down the road, into traffic.
He looked at me a long time.
I felt a churning
sickness in my belly
like a river freezing over.
I began to cry.

The streetlights ignited like
multitudinous buds.
I don't know how long
he had been
holding my hand.

Dermot J Archer

CHURCH GOING

Here is no *ruin-bibber*, no *Christmas-addict*
mass is standing room only; if you would understand
don't ask; take the road from the church
along dry stone walls, note how the small hardies become the cornerstones,
   wind musicians and jugglers.

As you enter Sheskinmore machair
tread softly, wild orchids sanctify here:
marsh, spotted, pyramidal, helleborine, twayblade;
where they give way to a glen of bracken,

Look up! The mass rock stencilled against the sky.

And you decide to climb. Archive a silent people,
nods and winks for time and place,
one hundred and forty years of sign language,
their native tongue whored.

That smell! Orchid perfume musked by smoky coconut
from a distant gorse fire could be
incense misting from a thurible;
murmuration carried in the wind
the sound of a congregation reciting Latin liturgy.

As the greenery becomes more lush
pause for a breathless meditation
behind you the sea,
eternally its sermon – Gravity.

Waving fronds freeze, scout eyes, morse code ears
of rabbits sense a look-out,
it's only a fox, his eyes sharp
sharper than the lens of a paparazzo.

Nearing the top, you might mistake a gorse petal
tapered by sunlight for a candle guttering in the breeze;
as a depressed cloud eclipses the sun
you imagine a figure in soutane
bowing to blow out the flame –
a signal to the soldier lying in wait.

The *Final Blessing* was yours.

Arun Sood

THE CORRAN FERRY

Gently bobbing,
the coal-glow Caledonian
vessel rumbles forwards
spraying damp specks
of faintly salted nostalgia
onto numb cheeks.

The Corran Ferry,
that decompression chamber
with one ramp to the city
and another to Gaga's cottage,
where winkles are chewed before supper
and hot water bottles placed within my bed.

Gabriel Rosenstock

CUIMHNE AR LIAM Ó MUIRTHILE

An chéad uair a bhuaileas le Liam Ó Muirthile (1950-2018) ba i mbialann
Choláiste na hOllscoile i gCorcaigh é. Bhí roinnt dánta aige ina ghlac,
aistriúcháin a dhein sé ar an bhfile Francach Jacques Prévert. Ag lorg
mo thuairime mar gheall orthu a bhí sé. Thugas uchtach dó. 'Tá siad
ar fheabhas, a bhuachaill!,' arsa mise leis. Agus bhí. I ndeireadh a oilith-
reachta ar an saol seo, thosnaigh sé ag cur suime arís, mar aistritheoir, i
bhfilíocht na Fraincise, go háirithe filíocht 'Négritude' choilíneachtaí is
iarchoilíneachtaí na Fraince.

Is gá é seo a rá – file domhanda ina dhearcadh ab ea an Muirthileach,
duine ilchultúrtha – duine ar gheal leis gach paróiste in Éirinn ach nach
dtaobhódh leis an bparóisteachas go deo. Aithne file ar fhile eile a bhí
agamsa ar Liam agus nuair a d'iarr sé orm Béarla a chur ar a chuid dánta,
thoilíos láithreach – agus le paisean! – mar gur theastaigh uaim go gcloisfí
a ghlór suaithinseach i bhfad is i gcéin. Chuamar chun na hIndia le chéile
agus roinneas na haistriúcháin a dheineas ar dhánta Liam le haos dána na
tíre sin. Scríobh duine acu chugam, Anand Thakore: 'Been enjoying your
translations of Liam's poems immensely – they're utterly direct, lyrical
and convincing '. Ar iarratas uaimse d'aistrigh Liam dánta leis an bhfile
Sitanshu Yashaschandra don díolaim *Briathar á Dhéanamh as Anáil*agus
bhuaileadar lena chéile nuair a bhí Liam thall san India.

Bhí an-áthas orm nuair a d'iarr Liam Carson, stiúrthóir IMRAM, ar an
Muirthileach a bheith mar aistritheoir ar an iliomad togra i gcaitheamh
na mblianta, amhráin Jacques Brel cuir i gcás, á gcanadh le gus ag Hilary
Bow agus Doimnic Mac Giolla Bhríde. Theastaigh uainn ligint orainn
go raibh cónaí orainn i dtír a mbeadh seónna den sórt sin mar ghnáthlón
cultúrtha ag daoine. Níl aon rud cearr leis an aisling sin, an bhfuil?

Thugas duine ilchultúrtha ar Liam: duine ilchumasach ab ea é dá réir,
mar fhile, mar iriseoir, mar úrscéalaí, mar dhrámadóir, mar chraoltóir
agus mar chriticeoir. Is trua, ar go leor bealaí, nár iarradh air i bhfad níos
mó aistí critice a scríobh. Féach ar an abairt seo, mar shampla, as *A New
View of the Irish Language* (Cois Life, 2008):

> In the world of poetry in Irish – a compass without co-ordinates – each
> poet marks out an individual point without making the compass whole.

Tá éirim neamhchoitianta san abairt sin agus san aiste sin uaidh ar an
nuafhilíocht trí chéile. Sa leabhar deireanach a tháinig óna pheann,
Camino de Santiago (Cois Life, 2018), dánta beaga glé i nGaeilge, Béarla,
Spáinnis agus Gailísis, dánta a neartóidh a cháil a thuilleadh mar fhile

agus mar fhear ilchultúrtha, tá dán ceithre líne dar teideal 'Slí Eile':

> Slí eile a ghabhas riamh
> a chruthaigh a comharthaíocht féin;
> slí nár léir i gcónaí a brí,
> slí filí.

Teistiméireacht ó fhíorfhile is ea é sin, teanntás agus féinamhras fite fuaite ina chéile. Seáp a thugamar faoin dtír roinnt blianta ó shin chun freastal ar léiriú ar dhráma de chuid Chathail Uí Shearcaigh, chuir sé ionadh an domhain orm an cur amach a bhí ag Liam ar an mbóthar agus ar stair na gceantar a ngabhamar tríothu. Ar ndóigh, ba chuid de thraenáil na bhfilí fadó é eolas domhain a chur ar an dinnseanchas.

Bhí fiosracht iontach ag baint le Liam, mar is dual d'iriseoir agus mar is dual d'ealaíontóir araon. Bhí dánta as a mhórchnuasach *An Fuíoll Feá* á dtaifeadadh againn i stiúideo Iarla Uí Lionáird agus lá dúinn ar an mbóthar baineadh stangadh asainn beirt: an boc seo ar thaobh an bhóthair agus sionnach beo ar a ghualainn aige. B'éigean dúinn stopadh láithreach agus forrán a chur ar an neach aisteach sin. B'in scéal Liam: bhí scéal éigin an-suimiúil ann i gcónaí, pé áit a mbeifeá, ach stopadh agus fios fátha an scéil a lorg.

Bhí sé lán de scéalta, lán de phleananna. Sa bhliain 2013 scríobh sé chugam mar a leanas:

> Cad déarfá le léamh poiblí a dhéanamh ar *An Choiméide Dhiaga* – Gaeilge, Iodáilis, Béarla – mar mhír ar chlár Imram 2014?

Bhuel, níor tharla an ócáid sin. Ná a lán ócáidí eile. Ach tharla méid áirithe, bí cinnte de – agus beidh Éire buíoch díot, a Liam! Shiúil tú an tslí a bhí romhat, mar a scríobhais sa leabhar deireanach uait, an féirín gleoite deireanach a fuaireas uait, *Camino de Santiago*:

> Tá sé ar fad romhainn
> ar an tslí.
>
> Guím
> go n-éireod gach lá le fonn
> tabhairt faoi,
>
> is mura bhfuil fonn féin orm
> nach ngéillfead aon lá
> don lagbhrí.

Turas na slí.
La amháin sa turas
iomlán mo ghuí.

Áiméan!

Ar *Tuairisc.ie* a foilsíodh é seo ar dtús

Gabriel Rosenstock

REMEMBERING LIAM Ó MUIRTHILE

I first met Liam Ó Muirthile (1950 -2018) in the refectory of UCC. He was clutching some neatly typed versions in Irish of the French poet, Jacques Prévert. He seemed anxious to know what I thought of them. "They're grand!" I said. And they were. A Francophile from an early age, he would devote much energy in recent years to translating the poetry of 'Négritude' and other works from the French colonies and former colonies. We look forward to all of this and to further posthumous titles, including his Rimbaud.

It's important to state that Ó Muirthile was global in outlook and multicultural by temperament and while he delighted in the geography, culture, literature, and lore of every county of Ireland – especially Kerry and Cork – no one could accuse him of being provincial or parochial.

I was delighted to be the main translator of his major bilingual collection *An Fuíoll Feá* (Cois Life, 2013) – a hectic few months producing a frisson between us that created many new poems in turn, poems that might not otherwise have come into being, poems in which Liam seemed to explore a landscape, skyscape, and seascape that struck me as ancient, timeless, precolonial, as well as unearthing levels of his own psyche.

We shared quite a few poetic peregrinations together and I was happy to get the chance to introduce him to audiences in India. One Mumbai-based poet, Anand Thakore, wrote to me saying, 'Been enjoying your translations of Liam's poems immensely – they're utterly direct, lyrical and convincing.' In India he met such poets as Sitanshu Yashaschandra, whom he had translated into Irish for an anthology I had prepared *Briathar á Dhéanamh as Anáil,* based on Dileep Jhaveri's anthology of Gujarati poetry, *Breath Becoming a Word.*

Liam Carson, Director of the IMRAM festival, roped him in to translate songs, such as those of Jacques Brel and Édith Piaf, and those who were fortunate enough to attend a performance won't easily forget how Hilary Bow and Doimnic Mac Giolla Bhríde breathed musical life into those Gaelic-Gallic texts. Encore!

Those of us associated with IMRAM wanted to believe that such cultural fare could be something we might come to expect amid a variety of cultural entertainments available in a capital city. Nothing much wrong with that vision, is there?

I've said he was multicultural; he was, concomitantly, multi-talented as poet, novelist, dramatist, broadcaster, columnist, and critic. We didn't get enough of his criticism; his measured thoughts on modern poetry in Irish, found in *A New View of the Irish Language* (Cois Life, 2008), are worth a second look:

> In the world of poetry in Irish – a compass without coordinates – each
> poet marks out an individual point without making the compass whole.

The most recent title of his arrived shortly before his death, *Camino de Santiago* (Cois Life, 2018), radiant, meditative lyrics in Irish, English, Spanish, and Galician – so much more interesting by dint of not being part of Ireland's wearisome monoglottism:

Slí eile a ghabhas riamh	I've always followed another way
a chruthaigh a comharthaíocht féin;	with signs of its own,
slí nár léir i gcónaí a brí,	often difficult to convey,
slí filí.	the way of the poem.
– 'SLÍ EILE'	– 'ANOTHER WAY'

A poet's testimony: confidence and self-doubt finely stitched together. On one of our road trips together – to see an amateur production of Cathal Ó Searcaigh's *Salomé* – I was astounded by Liam's knowledge of the countryside we traversed. There were few if any visible signs of Gaelic Ireland before the age of Swift, but old poets were speaking to Liam from the dim past, poets who wouldn't dare call themselves such without a knowledge of *dinnseanchas*.

He had curiosity in spades, a willingness to probe, essential if you are a journalist or an artist. On another occasion we were on the road to record poems from *An Fuíoll Feá* in Iarla Ó Lionáird's studio – chickens in the yard would add their unasked-for accompaniment – and Liam had to stop the car when we saw this bucko on the side of the road with a live fox on his shoulder. What's the story here for God's sake?

There was always a story. A laugh. And a tear. He could be a raucous vulgarian or a big softy as the situation required. His interest in language was as enormous as his appetite for it and he believed that Máire Mhac an tSaoi's uncle, Monsignor Pádraig de Brún, who translated Homer from ancient Greek and Dante from medieval Italian, should move up a place or two in the Gaelic pantheon. In 2013 he wrote to me suggesting a multilingual public reading of de Brún's *Divine Comedy*. That didn't happen, like a lot of other things. But so much did happen and we won't forget you, Liam, or the road you travelled:

Tá sé ar fad romhainn	It all lies before us
ar an tslí.	on the way.
Guím	I pray
go n-éireod gach lá le fonn	that I may arise each day
tabhairt faoi,	to willingly walk the way,

is mura bhfuil fonn féin orm
nach ngéillfead aon lá
don lagbhrí.

Turas na slí.
Lá amháin sa turas
iomlán mo ghuí.
        – 'AN TSLÍ'

and if I don't feel up to it
at least let me not give in
to unwillingness.

To walk the way,
one day at a time –
this my only prayer.
        – 'THE WAY'

Todo se extiende ante nosotros
en el camino.

Pido
que cada día me levante con ganas
de emprenderlo,

y si no tengo ánimo
que al menos no me rinda
al desánimo.

Caminar.
Día a día
es todo lo que pido.
        – 'EL CAMINO'

Todo está diante de nós
no camiño.

Só pido
que cada día me erge con arelas
de emprendelo,

e se non teño ganas
que polo menos non me renda
ao desánimo.

Camiñar.
Día a día
é todo o que pido.
        – 'O CAMIÑO'

Áiméan!

Liam Ó Muirthile

CAD É

Táim ó sheomra go seomra
ar fud an tí
ag lorg rud éigin,
is nach mbeidh a fhios agam
cad é nó
go bhfaighidh mé é.

Ní hé an stán aráin é
an plúr garbh donn
ná an plúr mín bán,
cé go dtógaim amach iad
is go gcuirim sa mheá iad
is go ndeinim builín amháin.

Ní haon leabhar a bhíos a léamh é
más buan mo chuimhne
is a leagas uaim,
cé go seasaím ag na seilfeanna
is go bhféachaim tríothu
is go dtéim ar mo ghlúine ar an urlár.

Ní haon eochair a bhí uaim í
ní rabhas ag dul amach
níor fhágas aon ní ar siúl,
cé go bhfuilim ó sheomra go seomra
ar fud an tí
ag lorg rud éigin
is nach faic é
is go bhfuilim ag déanamh bróin chiúin.

– from *An Fuíoll Féa* (Cois Life, 2013)

Kiera McGarry

PANTOUM FOR THE WAKE IN BALLYSTRUDDER

Your absence was an invitation:
friends and relatives kept coming as if to fill the house –
came knocking with biscuit hampers, canned meats, cold casseroles.
Spring's first lambs eased out their bleats over your fields.

Friends and relatives kept coming as if to fill the house.
We hugged and kissed them, cooked pots of tea.
Spring's first lambs eased out their bleats over your fields,
while we ate feasts of tea-logged biscuits and reheated casseroles

and felt empty. The top-end of the table persisted plateless.
The rooms were silent: this was the song of your new country.
Your old dog lapped the jelly feebly from her dinner of canned meats
then curled up in the hall, cold and grey as a haunch.

The rooms were silent. This was the song of your old country,
sounding in our heads: that of seed-eating barley-sparrows, bleating ewes
bedded down in the barn, heavy and dense as storm-bearing clouds.
I could imagine them, and the others, coming too –

the cows braying for your bucket by the garden gate, sheep scrambling
across strewn flowerbeds, and the yard horse come knocking,
prop-hoofed with her dreams of a clapped shoulder.
Your absence is their invitation.

Lynn Harding

SOUTH TERRACE

(i)

That sweet, smoky smell
slick grit of oil and rubber
on terracotta diamonds
the absence of spring cleaning
or any other season's.

A hopeful child tests the bells on
all the pink and purple bicycles
she will never own.
Behind, the workshop is decked out
in coloured potions
poisons marked with Xs
clear to even
the smallest of girls
busy building a cardboard castle
dungeons hoarding ball bearings.

Downstairs, her dad guards the coffers
never empty
but never full.

(ii)

It was a wonder
how you balanced it all
on the cycle across town:
schoolbag, violin, daydreams
my whole world
while yours was perched upon the crossbar
curls flying
feeling invincible.

I never felt the cost of a sale
or saw the old man before you;
only your name above the door
the first one I learned to speak.

James Harpur

SCRIBE B
— from 'Kells'

> *'Writing blurs your eyes, gives you a stoop, stabs your ribs and stomach,*
> *makes your kidneys throb and afflicts your whole body.'*
> — Florentius, 10th-century Iberian scribe

Words copied in rage, blotch.
Words written in silence
can still be full of noise.

What use a holy book
that can't deter the teeth of mice,
or bite of swords?

My face says: *Ecce, nemo!*
My heart burns for praise.

If God needs witnesses
for his creation, *why* such a sin
to want the same for mine?

Fleck of froth
on waves of scribal duties.

Another endless
day of endless
rows of endless
words.

Cassiodorus says: writing inflicts
a wound on Satan.
Who is wounding me?

The open door —
stars of daisies,
a dandelion sun;
only the air between us.

How strange
that ink-strokes

when left unguided
find a way to draw
wild flowers
between the lines?

Outside: wagtails, bees,
whitethorn, hazel.
Inside: nibs, liquid soot.

Gary Allen

EDDIE AND THE GOAT

My uncle was more Eddie Cochran than Elvis
though he could slick his brilliantined hair back
and do a shuffle when singing, *Well, it's One for the money, Two for the show*

especially on Friday night when he was washing his bones
at the Belfast sink in the kitchen.

He loved sugar – my uncle, that is –
bags of sweets, Wall's ice cream that came silver wrapped
and separate from the castle-shaped cone
and even rough tea leaves mixed with sugar
in the palm of his hand.

While the striped sun curtain billowed in the doorway
Elvis and Eddie and the Beatles shouted from the turntable
of the case-carrying playing machine
accompanied by the screaming voices of half a dozen children.

Eddie is the greatest, as he sprung his band stick – my uncle, that is –
high into the clouds in the yards,
pure rock and roll, like a Saturday night ballroom
or an Orange parade through a shower of stones and glass.

Art Ó Súilleabháin

THE HOROLOGIST

Papers in the back of an old drawer
tied with a cracked rubber band
burst out of their bundles
when I found them,
almost bromide,
perhaps they were white once.

They were dated 1950, weekly:
notes, diagrams, exercises,
showing jewels as axes,
rockers, springs,
steel or brass,
'how' to rewind or reset them.

Notched wheels fitted each other
snugly, turn and link, gearing
to mark time in the turning,
hands revolving
from spindles
within rounded or oval casings.

Teachings to repair small workings,
things to be read and practised,
work a correspondence,
a distance education
from your era,
your way up, your chance to shine.

But when the time came for exams
a trip to Dublin cost too much,
papers stowed, like learning.
You didn't go,
you stayed,
you saved the hay and cut the turf.

I remember you, eyeglass firmly set,
poring over the innards of another
time-piece that counted wrong,
the cog-filled maze

deciphered, fixed.
"That one is ready for Máirtín Tom."

You sat at one end of the kitchen table,
two boxes of watch-parts scattered
on a double page of the *Tribune*.
All that remains
is in the shed
left in the back of an old drawer.

They were my attempt at poems once,
neatly arranged in plastic pockets,
bursting with archaic words,
when she finds them,
stuck together,
papers in the back of an old drawer.

Ben Dombroski

WHITE NOISE MACHINE: WHALES

The whales are moving northward together
from their calving grounds in the gulf.
Calves with the larger ones, like flaws
in a sheet of glass – small fissures
that leak a kind of deeper light.
They cover thirty miles a day
like that, to where my father writes
he's spotted a pod of them
from the hill above the place he's rented
in Wellfleet. All summer, he says,
they'll come to feed on haddock
and squid before heading south again
to breed. It's the most I've heard in months:
whales tracing the coasts – the sea-isles,
capes and bays that lie between us.
In the other room, my daughter
lies in her crib, and through the monitor
I listen to the noise machine
she needs to sleep loop the whistles
and clicks and pulsed calls that give each
a shape in the others' minds. She's down now,
and I'm the restless one, crossing
and re-crossing the hall to watch
her breathing in the dark. It's late.
A heat already hangs on the night,
and even the insects have abandoned
their choruses beneath street lights
in the alleys. I listen again
at the door to her breathing as if
underwater – like a diver sent down
in her bell to explore a wreck,
salvage whatever there is of worth.

Peter Sirr

DISREGARD EVERYTHING

Douglas Dunn, *The Noise of a Fly* (Faber and Faber, 2017), £14.99.
Andrew Motion, *Essex Clay* (Faber and Faber, 2018), £14.99.
David Harsent, *Salt* (Faber and Faber, 2017), £14.99.

Douglas Dunn has been such a notable part of the poetry landscape that
it's surprising to realise that this is his first book for sixteen years. Maybe
because we don't expect poets to retire we assume the volumes will continue to arrive punctually, uninterruptedly – an expectation Dunn himself
is happy to play with, including mocking the self-repetition that can come
with old age: 'Gave yet another lecture. God, I'm boring. / Said all the
same old things I've said before' ('Thursday'). Well, what of it? that poem
goes on to say. The point is to carry on, and this book is just that, a glad
carrying on of the obligation to respond to whatever life throws up.

Imperfection and loss are, necessarily, everywhere. The fly of the
title, along with a myriad other interruptions – '*A memory of yesterday's
pleasures, a feare of to morrows dangers, a straw under my knee, a noise in mine
ear, a light in mine eye, an any thing*' – is a disturbance of the impulse to the
spiritual as experienced by John Donne in the sermon extract that serves
as epigraph. It's an acceptance of imperfection (the 'Just-cleaned window
now smeared with dove-shit' from 'The Nothing-But'), as well as a pro-
motion of purposeful idleness, as in the poem of that title:

> Can you hear them? The flap of a butterfly.
> The unfolding wing of a resting wren.
> The sigh of an exhausted garden-ghost.
> A poem trapped in an empty fountain pen.

Age and mortality feature heavily, and the tone of the book as a whole
is elegiac. These are poems of old age, looking age and its depredations
– physical and cognitive decline, the prospect of outliving your own intel-
lect – squarely in the eye.

> ... No one
> looks forward to being old and alone,
> The carer with a spoon,
> Visitor gone,
> Boredom and fright on television.
> How do you understand the merry young

As you endure a dragging afternoon
With a hundred names on the tip of your tongue,
Unable to cheer yourself up,
In a constant state of indecision?

– 'REMEMBERING FRIENDS WHO FEARED OLD AGE AND DEMENTIA
MORE THAN DEATH'

To which the only possible answer is 'Cheers! Let's pour another cup.'
Some of the poems are a reluctant leavetaking of the working life of the
poet-academic, 'Not pushed, but oh-so-very-gently shoved / Towards
the book-loaded van and a pension'; rueful reflections – 'Young women,
and young men, I, too, was young'; or the chastened self-examination
and scrutiny of the artistic impulse, as in the excellent poem about Rem-
brandt's self-portraits:

How do you write about yourself? How do you say,
'I do not like the way I have become,'
And not feel stupid?

One of the dubious privileges of age is the right to dispense advice. The
older artist, after a lifetime of practice, gets to parade his expertise and lay
down the law:

Think in pictures. Think in rhythm. Then let
Other see and hear them too. Don't forget
Poetry can oblige you to be insolent …

–'A TEACHER'S NOTES'

After a string of edicts, though, this particular instructor has the grace to
conclude 'Now, disregard everything I've written', with the further useful injunction to stay off the pot noodles and learn how to cook.

Other highlights of a rich collection include 'The House of the Blind',
'Near Myths', and the long poem where he considers his own particular
language choice, 'English (a Scottish Essay)'. One of the most attractive
poems is a memory of a tramp whose travel routes were based on 'a
handed-on / Knowledge of havens and hostels', and which amount to
'An Alternative Map of Scotland'.

Andrew Motion's new collection revisits the familiar, obsessive terrain
of his mother's death as a result of a riding accident, and deals also with
his father's death, and his meeting after forty years with the girlfriend he
was visiting at the time of his mother's accident. A single long poem in
three parts, in form it's strikingly plain, a straightforward narrative presented in very lightly punctuated and spatially varied free verse, lineated
according to emphasis or emotional force. The effect is often dramatic,

partly stemming from the decision to relate the account in the third person with the point of view limited to the time when these events are unfolding. The resulting distance allows the poet a kind of forensic presentation and examination that might otherwise prove awkwardly confessional. It also precludes the kind of after the event reflection that would dilute the immediacy Motion has settled on as his primary instrument. This is also the method of the prose memoir *In the Blood*, first published in 2006 and reissued to coincide with *Essex Clay*. That book narrates the poet's very upper-class English childhood up to the point of his mother's riding accident while fox-hunting. She was in a coma for three years and didn't die for several years after that. She was the emotional centre of the poet's life – the father is a more distant figure, not much given to speech or overt affection – and the effect of the accident on him is shattering. The poem succeeds brilliantly in conveying the numbing stages of grief:

> Grief.
>   too little a word
>   no spring-lock inside it
> primed
>   to snap back to its opposite

The directness, the lack of apparent artifice, all intensify the focus and keep the narrative's record of unbearable loss building relentlessly. It's as if the poet has decided that given the intensity of the material itself, a serviceable prose can be made to carry the weight or emotional heft of poetry. Yet every word, every space, every break, is carefully considered, meticulously weighted; there is in fact plenty of artifice. Detail is everything: the poem works by the accretion of telling details, intense observation of landscape or significant encounter:

> The intact frost of early morning
>   and a blade of ice
>   drawn from the tap in the stable yard.

Or, as he meets his beloved Juliet:

> Her black hair   black
>   not a black enough word.
>
> Her red mouth.
>
> Her skin white   but mainly full
>   ripeness.
>
> And she is looking straight at him.

Or again, as he sits in the train on his way to visit his dying father:

> ... the draggle and widening light
>> above childhood flatlands
>>> that still bewitch him
> with their marvellous corals
>> and Elvis-quiffed fish

The ideal experience might be to read the prose memoir and the poetic sequel together, but *Essex Clay* works perfectly convincingly as a standalone piece, one of Motion's best books to date.

David Harsent is a fecund and inventive poet, and *Salt* is his eleventh collection. He's the kind of poet who can seemingly write about anything. A random commission to write a poem based on a Royal Institute lecture title led, to his own surprise, to the brilliant *Legion*, his 2005 collection on war. His last collection, *Fire Songs*, winner of the TS Eliot Prize, foregrounded his dark, apocalyptic vision, opening with a terrifying account of the burning of the martyr Anne Askew. He has said of his own work that its default mode is dark, which is fair enough, but *Salt* is less overtly desolate than some of the previous work. It's a curious creature: a long book, at almost 180 pages, consisting of a set of untitled short poems, 'a series, not a sequence' (Harsent is very much a 'serial' poet, favouring loose connections over rigorous orchestration), in which salt is a linking motif. Focus or coherence aren't the point, so it would be silly to look for them. In spite of the linkages and echoes, the pleasures are local to the individual poems.

The author's note makes clear that each poem operates independently but that, as they were written, 'some loose, disjointed narratives' developed, though the second part of his descriptions is closer: 'small, broken chains of hint and harmony'. The real unity derives from the dream-like world the poems share, with its 'Mirrors set at angles' and voices carrying 'from one image to the next'. That and the even, flattened or restrained tone that all the poems share and which stems, in turn, from the poems' improvisatory nature, the sense that they've been plucked from the air, that lines and images are run with to see what might ensue, what might catch and kindle. In spite of the foreboding and the sense of absence, unfulfilment and loss that haunt the poems, what often seems most at stake is the imagination's own ability to create a mood, formalise a fleeting notion or instinct – poetry itself is often the implied subject, with the poems extending their invitation to the reader to enjoy what they conjure:

> He calculated sadness, types of sadness, sadness by degree,
> the way a touch withdrawn might settle somewhere else.

Or,

> A through-draught in an empty house, a curtain lifting
> by a broken window, ash stirring in the grate, letters
> on a table rising and settling. He lived with the image for days.
> The letters were undated and the pen-work strong.

Or,

> They eavesdropped on one another. He read her mind.
> She wrote him notes that could have come from anyone.

Harsent has said in an interview, 'Poetry is a condensed form. It is much closer to music than to prose. If I can't hear the music, I don't think it is a poem.' In all of these poems the impulse of the music is clearly evident. The book is full of enviable lines; as I was reading it I was also reading Robert Hass's *A Little Book on Form*, where he reminds us of Lowell's famous statement that 'It's much easier to write a good poem than a good line', which would be even more brilliant if it were true, but you see what he means. Conversely, you can have too many good lines that seem to cry out for a convincing poem to find themselves in. Harsent's book is full of the pleasure of individual lines and images but it can seem a little affectless, without the pressure or urgency that fires his best work.

Mark Baker

THE SCARECROW

The road is its own wind,
its stations and signposts in the crows
observing the vast contribution of the leaves,
the run of grain in down-pouring chutes,
good deeds foraged
with wisdom no more than a coat in a field,
a sleeve reached-for
when what mouses in and darts,
quickens in the rind of situations, makes courage start.
I stood and stared but the bonfire-builders returned
with petrol thrown into the sunset
brought to the brink of another grand escape,
trees were bars through which it went
opening then closing widely,
bigger than I was,
that could take my weight
for their look-outs, stashes, sparks, glee;
they thought there were better ways,
the older ones,
the glamour-keepers,
than the post-surgical turnip the crow-man gave me
for a face.

Linda Opyr

WHERE THE EYE WANTS COAST

Autumn shares its branches with both sun and frost
and I don't know what the day will bring.

But I do know that we come ashore
both with and against the tide.

And that same solemn rain that follows us home
says nothing of when or if it will return.

Here is where the tale begins:

A scrim of fog where the eye wants coast.
Someone seeks harbour. Someone sets sail.

They wave in their passing.
Their longing, one and the same.

John W Sexton

THE OWNERSHIP OF THE YELLOW PURSE

> after *I Screathan An Cheoigh*
>   by Eoghan Rua Ó Súilleabháin (1748–1782)

On my way through foggy Scrathan
– hoping to step into brand new boots –
I met a woman, beautiful and weeping,
rooting in the pasture through the grassy roots.
>   Monday's market, Monday's market,
>   Monday's market – oh that yellow purse.
>   It is well lost now for Monday's market;
>   for I'm blinded by tears that hinder my search.

I would rather waste a crown in the local pub
than the golden purse I mislaid last night.
It was a gift given me by that handsome fob,
jiggling his hips to the fiddle in flight.
>   Monday's market, Monday's market,
>   Monday's market – oh that yellow purse.

O sensible and learned O'Brien, O'Brien the Mirthful;
canny, world-travelled, Steadfast O'Brien the Generous!
It is my wish and longing to seek out your counsel,
to find out what happened to my yellow purse.
>   Monday's market, Monday's market,
>   Monday's market – oh that yellow purse.

Ovid owned it – pulled from it his flawless measure;
Homer dipped his quill in it, a golden well.
From its bounty Maol enticed another man's lover;
for that he was chased over ocean's swell.
>   Monday's market, Monday's market,
>   Monday's market – oh that yellow purse.

Dido had it, displayed across her breasts;
many a man put in coins, but none were taken.
Diana had it, and Oh! Wasn't she the minx!
Its glare in the forest set off a conflagration.
>   Monday's market, Monday's market,
>   Monday's market – oh that yellow purse.

Diarmaid, once undefeated, he also owned it;
but lost it during the hunt for the enchanted pig.
Diarmaid may have healed Iatach of a serpent's bite,
but Fionn would not give him even healing spit.
       Monday's market, Monday's market,
       Monday's market – oh that yellow purse.

It proved its advantage for Cearbhall Ó Dálaigh,
turning out churns, harrows, and boats for the King;
tin cans and hoops and wheels and whole barrels,
and turning the ladies with eloquent talking.
       Monday's market, Monday's market,
       Monday's market – oh that yellow purse.

Cearbhall's scythes could cut air into swatches.
He made hackle and carding comb, adze and sword,
thunderous blunderbusses and waistcoat watches,
and pins for ladies that were the final word.
       Monday's market, Monday's market,
       Monday's market – oh that yellow purse.

It was a fine treasure indeed within Noah's Ark,
as the ship held solid on the tip of each wave;
and every beast and every yelping, screech and bark,
held tight in that purse till they landed safe.
       Monday's market, Monday's market,
       Monday's market – oh that yellow purse.

Jason also had it as a brief possession –
it was far more convenient than that blasted Fleece.
For a while Paris had it, ransomed to his passion,
till blood flowed in Troy and ancient Greece.
       Monday's market, Monday's market,
       Monday's market – oh that yellow purse.

Great was its time at sea with the Fair Merchant;
its endless bounty meant he could trade what he liked.
Dúnlaing also had it, his face hidden in wool raiment;
he severed arteries and futures with a precious pike.
       Monday's market, Monday's market,
       Monday's market – oh that yellow purse.

Clíodhna had it, while in our Land-above-Water,
as she travelled at night in a wine-cask.
Aoife had it, the children of Lir's wicked stepmother –
and they on the Moyle serving their three hundred years.
>   Monday's market, Monday's market,
>   Monday's market – oh that yellow purse.

Deirdre had it once, in which she kept her chessmen,
and all who loved her fell then to the sword.
Samson had it, and when he was shorn found strength within.
And Bacchus had it too; hence, the wine flowed.
>   Monday's market, Monday's market,
>   Monday's market – oh that yellow purse.

The Great Eejit had it, when in thrall to the wife of the Enchanter,
who was rumoured then to have her fingers in it.
Macha of the Red Mane possessed it, and it gave fierce power;
even swords would bleed at the sight of it.
>   Monday's market, Monday's market,
>   Monday's market – oh that yellow purse.

It was a great boon to that German, Fortunatus.
He delved his hand in deep, unafraid of wealth,
and granted the ladies coins and gold trinkets.
May it never empty, but be forever full to its depth.
>   Monday's market, Monday's market,
>   Monday's market – oh that yellow purse.

Mitchelstown, O Mitchelstown, drinking down the liquor,
I saw my yellow purse last night, bright as wet.
Peddlers' wives and tinkers' wives, I saw them clear:
leaping and a'lepping, dancing the Yellow Coverlet.
>   Monday's market, Monday's market,
>   Monday's market – a rich curse!
>   No Monday's market, no market yet,
>   for my heart was poured into that yellow purse.

Jane Robinson

MATERIALS REQUIRED

Gun,
neatsfoot oil from shinbones and feet but not the hooves,
an inflorescence of blue,
broken hacksaw blade,
the stitching finger,
strontium yellow or barium yellow,
massicot mixed with sugar candy,
formaldehyde,
luck.

Frank Ormsby

THE SOUND OF TRAINS
– *NY*

The trains have a different rush and a different cry
in the gully behind the houses.
Sometimes, heard from a distance, they are the sound
of a Manhattan summer, boiling in the sun.
Closer, a cemetery runs beside them for miles.
Here they utter their redemptive holler,
as though the Angel Gabriel were on board,
as though they had shaped a special cry to greet
a field of tombstones. Sometimes, in the small hours,
they are a flute tuning up, or the opening wail
of a harmonica, but they never get beyond the first note
of their threnody for bruised spirits,
a drawn-out blues, as I imagine it, that picks up words
in box-cars among the hoboes, and in the long trains
that take an age to worm out of town. They arouse the dark
more than the ticking lust of cicadas. Alone at our windows,
or blessed with company, we will never get used to the trains'
faint undercurrent of alarm, the way each leaves,
briefly, in the air, its different rush and cry,
how each, with its hoarse flair and yearning fall,
announces its passing.

Patrick Kehoe

WHAT REMAINS AFTER THE WIND

What remains after the wind
Has blown away our words:
An ordinary street, pin sharp stars.

To make myth of a particular street
Its ache and pang – a friend in Spain
Looks at a photograph and writes:
'So maybe this is not the place at all,
It would be further back down the street.'

Maybe this is not the place at all ...
And his words echo
Down the street recalled.

Robyn Rowland

THAT TOGETHER, WE WENT

that we went out, the neighbours,
one deaf since birth, alive to music and words,
chock-full of imagination,
the other intelligent and curious.

that we went out, friends,
along the connemara shoreline with its jagged hurt,
its timeless stories of lost roofs off houses,
stone-walled gables standing alone now.

that we went out
to the local hotel, new and about to struggle
that held its opening, and we went,
past the ragged houses and the early evening.

that coming home together with a glass too many,
road along the shoreline bending and swaying
like old Dylan songs they had played,
and against the still-high sun at late evening

one cow stock-still on the ridge of hill near home
a glaze of tangerine sky on its rump
and behind all blue, like that's what heaven is.
and knowing that this is the feeling that's best,

fluid old-fashioned thanks, almost in tears
for the friendship and the slow ways home
and the twilight, dripping orange and blue
under a three-quarter moon before summer.

Maser
Repeal the 8th (detail from triptych, 2018)
Spraypaint and acrylic on canvas, 100 x 100 cm (x 3)

X/M   *War changes its address - Aleppo*   Maguire '18

Brian Maguire
War Changes Its Address (2018)
Lithograph, 34 x 24 in

Dean Kelly
Did You Get Enough (2007)
Acrylic and mixed media, 16 x 16 in

Rita Duffy
Manifestation Study I (2003)
Oil on lead on panel, 12 x 12 in

Jennifer Cunningham
Nite Club (2018)
Mixed media, 30 x 22 inch

Will St Leger
Out of the Shadows (2017)
Mixed media

The images in this issue are from a recent exhibition, entitled 'Art of Protest',
at The Kenny Gallery, Galway (**www.thekennygallery.ie**)

Fred Johnston

WORLDS NEWMADE

Eamonn Lynskey, *It's Time* (Salmon Poetry, 2017), €12.
Kate Noakes, *Paris, Stage Left* (Eyewear Publishing, 2017), €12.99.
Dawn Wood, *Declaration* (Templar Poetry, 2016), £10.
Joan Newmann, *Dead End* (Summer Palace Press, 2018), €10.

The language of Eamonn Lynskey's poetry is of a sort that invites one
into the core of the poem as through an open door. Yet it is only when
one has begun to read and contemplate what is behind the door that one
sees incredible simple horrors; of violence, neglect, deep injustice, and a
calm nobility under pressure.

The human condition in the twenty-first century is not a pleasant one
and it is precarious. Lynskey is to be congratulated for reminding us that,
in some instances, our own small personal injustices and injuries are often
microcosms of big ones and our moral impotence in the face of them.

The title poem introduces us, through a door pushed open into a shed
full of garden implements, to the underlying tone of those that follow:

> When I creak the shed door open,
> shears and spade blink in the corner: come,
> the world must be newmade. It's time.

In 'Down to Africa', Lynskey suggests that, 'Earth will clothe herself
afresh, the way / she greened the terraces of Angkor Wat'; and when this
process is complete, it's back to the possibility of new human beginnings
in a natural circle back in the cradle of Africa. There's an odd comfort in
that. But murder and destruction is not a new thing: 'Warrior' conjures
up Ötzi, the mummified remains found in the Dolomite Alps some years
ago, which bear indications of death by a fired arrow; the narrator in the
poem, with professional detachment, proclaims that ...

> "... We have that unfortunate
> and not infrequent military
> occurence: death from friendly fire ..."

The camouflage phrases 'friendly fire', along with 'collateral damage',
must be two of the most obscene creations of the military mind. If one
were Catholic in Ireland, one was at war from childhood, in constant
danger of attack from a vague but savage foe, and the enemy was always
at the gates:

I try explaining to a grandchild

how we were conscripted in the war
against an enemy determined
to destroy us.

– 'SPEAKING OF THE PAST'

Our banners were 'pictures of the Sacred Heart', and our propaganda press comprised '*The Messenger* / brought home from school each month'. How many of us, one might ask, were victims of 'friendly fire' or merely 'collateral damage' in this invisible struggle?

A quite beautiful poem, entitled 'Metsu's Women', is a reflection of the paintings and short life of Dutch painter, Gabriel Metsu, a Baroque painter whose father was a painter and tapestry worker, and who died aged 38. His works, depicting mainly individuals at work or playing instruments, hunting, or writing, can be seen at Dublin's National Gallery, one of which is *Man Writing a Letter*:

Young blades write letters, cavaliers
press their attentions on young maidens,
huntsmen rest long-barrelled guns
at doorways, trade their fresh-skilled spoil
of birds and hares with servant girls.

More than a contemplation of the painter's work, it has the quiet quality of a lament in which Metsu's early demise is a poignant reminder of the lasting virtue of art over uncertain life itself. Fine poems throughout this collection ought to reinforce Lynskey's reputation. As a stylist, he could teach our younger catch of poets a thing or two. And he is never dull.

Kate Noakes's sixth collection lifts the curtain (sort of) on that ever-seductive city of Paris. A Welsh academic, she was born in Bristol and travels between Paris and London. Noakes came to Paris in 2011 chasing a job. *Paris, Stage Left* is a memory-compendium of her early days there. In this, Noakes dons the role of *flâneuse*. Paris excites, of course it does. Artists and poets have been fetching up there since time immemorial, and Hemingway's angst-drunk PR introduced a whole generation of young Americans to his idea of glorious artistic despair. Some years ago, this reviewer published a booklet of poems written in Paris (in English), *Paris Without Maps*; I remain much in love with the place.

Noakes ushers the reader onto the Métro, and makes poetic remarks about places and things as one rattles along. It's hard for any writer not native to a country to morph into anything more than a tourist, even with the passage of time. For the reader, a casual knowledge of French wouldn't hurt; for example, to know that *pelouse interdite* means 'Keep off the grass'. Noakes does also present a poem in English with its French translation, 'Shoulder to Shoulder':

> I do not ask why,
> I deny you understanding
>
> Je ne demande pas pourquoi
> Je vous nie compréhension

The book is set in three sections, 'History', 'Tragedy', and 'Comedy'. Noakes also 'channels' some well-known painters and even that gun-running young reprobate Rimbaud, with her poem 'Je suis une autre'. Rimbaud (whose name, by some accident of fate, rocks neatly with the word *'ribaud'*, French for a debauched person), actually argued 'Je est un autre', suggesting that the 'I' was another self, as it were. Noakes has feminised the gender of 'autre' here, referring the poem to herself:

> My mouth's full of cotton rags,
> I'm tone deaf.
> So, forgive me
> if all I can do today
> is hum a little, honey.

The poem 'When the Troubadour' is dedicated to the late Seamus Heaney, and, suitably, there are references to blackbirds, midwinter, and harbingers. It's not at all a bad poem, but like so many of the not-at-all-bad poems here, there is contained in it a weight of distance, a spectating, which reminds us of just how much like postcards or snap-shots travel poetry (surely a genre all its own) can be. Noakes takes us, then, through a personalised and re-imagined Paris in poems that are always crafted and intriguing, and with an engaging lightness of touch. All in all, a tasty *raisin flaugnarde.*

Templar Poetry, based in Derbyshire, also hosts the poetry magazine *iOTA*, and some other poetry-relevant items besides. Their books, like those of Eyewear Publishing, are beautifully produced, with attractive artwork in an unusual but pleasing format. They do justice to Omagh poet, Dawn Wood, for whom *Declaration* is a third collection, and who lives these days in Perthshire, Scotland. Are these 'religious' poems? There is a scent of the other-worldly as imagined by the Old Testament, the Psalms, and the Epic of Gilgamesh; chiefly, however, these marvel-lously-crafted poems, paying careful attention to rhythm and choice of language, preach nothing at the reader, but rather invite him or her to analyse their prophetic and devotional aspects for themselves.

The word of Yahweh, a command –
that emblem that extends come in,
my voice will train a hedge of sparrows!
speak your mind in peace.

– 'WAKE', AFTER PSALM 110

The collection is separated into four sections, 'The Dream of Utnapishtim', 'An Old Dog Speaks Morning', 'Choral', and 'Litany of a Cathedral'. 'Choral' comprises a series of well-honed sonnets revolving around Belfast, in one manner or other; 'Litany of a Cathedral' acts as a kind of map, pinned by sharp, aphoristic, four-line poems:

Man, playing out his part on cue,
as actor, called upon to do.
Blood as life – soliloquy –
how long was I so trained as you?

– 'CROSS'

But this is decidedly not a set of dry-as-dust meditations, there's humour here too, and observations on the ordinary. Above all, perhaps, there is considered and confident poetry here which neither bullies by yelling or seduces by whispering, but which invites us to observe and interpret and not take ourselves too seriously while we're at it. These poems are a celebration of the finite and the mystical, the knowable and the arcane. Was Utnapishtim really Noah? A fine collection by a competent and mature poet.

'If this is to be Newmann's last calling card – as it is suggested – then it is a powerhouse of a swansong.' So concluded a recent Lagan Online review of *Dead End*. One certainly hopes not. And one cannot be at all sure that this collection is indeed a 'swansong'. Born in 1942, Joan was a member of what became known as the 'Hobsbaum Group', at Queen's University, Belfast, and was contemporate there with James Simmons and Seamus Heaney. In 1999, Joan and her daughter Kate set up Summer Palace Press, out of a series of literary workshops and guest tutelage. Since then, they've published numerous collections of poetry. And with little financial support. The book's cover is featureless and there are none of the predictable blurbs of praise from tame poets on the back. Alas, this minimalism goes too far; there isn't even a table of contents. Inside the cover, there is a ghostlike photo of a child, obviously from an earlier age. And yes, most of the poems, whether making jokes dark or luminous, concern, well, death.

The Romans, no fools, posted a slave behind the imperator on his chariot when, on occasion, he was granted a triumph through Rome after success in battle. The slave's job was to whisper in the elevated victor's ear, 'Remember that thou art mortal', just to keep him grounded.

Newmann too is, perhaps, whispering in our ears with these poems.
She gets right into the entrails of the matter: death is out there. There is
no vote. We'd rather forget about it, especially if it's someone else's turn:

> A man left his dead mother seated
> in her favourite armchair.
>
> His mother died of natural causes
> in the chair in July 2005,
> aged ninety-two.
> [...]
> The man said, when interviewed,
> he could not face
> organising a funeral.
>
> – 'BEWARE OF THIS AND THAT'

'Simple Cremation' is essentially a list of things to do whilst preparing
for a cremation at Belfast's Roselawn Cemetery. (My own parents are
interred there, along with many victims of Northern Ireland's conflict).
This list includes a host of songs to be played. Joni Mitchell has a spot,
along with Jeff Buckley, Randy Newman, and the marvellous Antony and
the Johnsons, among others. Elsewhere there are nods to Dylan Thomas
and Peig Sayers, to Akhmatova and John Donne, to the much-missed
James Simmons, and to Samuel Johnson, Pushkin, and John Brown of
Harpers Ferry fame. And Salvador Dali. and Orwell. And Jonathan Swift.
And Andrew Marvell. Some of the poems lilt gracefully into songs. This
isn't dark and forbidding stuff, it's celebratory, and a paean to literature's
greatest hits. The final poem is 'Life':

> Touch
>
> and
>
> go.

And so the gig finishes. But the poems demand reading and re-reading.
They are neither as simplistic nor as throw-away as one or two may
indicate. They are funny, sad, thoughtful, and entrancing. They utilise a
free-form linguistic candidness that probably makes them ideal for reciting
aloud. They are vigorous and oddly reassuring.

Life-affirming, one might say.

Oliver Mort

THE NUMBER 61 BUS
  – for Frank Ormsby

Midway on the journey
of the 61 Bus.

A dolorous drive down from Carr's Glen
to the Cavehill Road,
downwards on past the Westland,
the Waterworks park
and the Limestone Road.

Passengers waiting at bus stops
in the morning darkness.
Waiting on their return journey
on a road to nowhere.
The city centre.

And you sitting somewhere on
that same death drive
like Virgil.

Able to show me small miracles
taking flight out the window.
The angry man standing
in his own dog's shit.
Cursing his mutt called Beatrice.

Shannon Kelly

KINTSUGI

I remember the day that men stopped noticing me,
she says, her hands folded and two coffees between us.
Oh they still notice, she says, but for different reasons,
not so good reasons, lonely reasons. Her eyes trace old years
of skinny jeans and David Bowie and her father,
who beat her, bloodied up her face, sent her staggering
out of the house limping, always follows them with But I loved him,
I did. Someday, I will write this into a poem, she says, someday
when I forget the taste of vomit, I will write this down. That day,
I won't be afraid of what daddy will think or say. I am waiting
for my fears to disappear, she tells me. I am sitting in my house
alone, listening to the sounds of nesting in the eves, I am rocking
myself and swallowing books and waiting for divine inspiration.
I am collecting all the bowls I crushed and mending them with gold,
with fire.

Martin Malone

BIDDEN
     after Mary Bordern

Here are cotton things
and rubber things;
here, liquids and pots.
Here are steel things
and pillows; tin boxes,
needles and glass.
Here, are labels and little
white squares of gauze.

Yes, I know
that you understand these things
but it doesn't do to think.

You pile blankets
onto his wasted body;
fetch jugs of hot water;
boil long rubber tubes
in wretched saucepans.

Their courtesy as they die,
reluctant to cause me trouble
or put me out, as I gauge
how fast a life is ebbing.

Some hurry,
chasing a last omnibus,
for others, there is no such rush,
as if savouring the slow throes
of their own obliteration.

His brain comes off in my hands
as I lift away the bandage,
Death annoyed at my fussing.

I know you understand,
but what have you
and all these things
to do with the dying
of this man?

Nothing.
Take them away.
Release has entered the room
and a miracle draws near.

Julie Hungiville LeMay

LOSING MY BROTHER

The snowstorm muffles the sky grey:
wind muzzled, sunlight deadened.
Mike says it's like London fog
and I have nothing to say to anyone.

He's fogged with morphine and a disease
that shatters body and bones.
Beard grizzled, mouth mumbled.

His arms jut out stick-like.
Pathology indicates aggressive
poorly differentiated malignancy.
It's everywhere.

Dad always said *You can't*
make wood out of ashes.
Mike says *It is what it is.*

Matthew Geden

THE ROADS THEY DREAM

Kevin Higgins, *Song of Songs 2.0: New and Selected Poems* (Salmon Poetry, 2017), €14.
Eamonn Wall, *Junction City: New and Selected Poems 1990-2015* (Salmon Poetry, 2015), €12.
Catherine Ann Cullen, *The Other Now: New and Selected Poems* (Dedalus Press, 2016), €12.50.

Satirical poetry in Ireland is not a new phenomenon. Even before Jonathan Swift there were plenty of literary examples, as illustrated by Roisin McLaughlin in her book, *Early Irish Satire*, published in 2008 by the School of Celtic Studies at the Dublin Institute for Advanced Studies. In more recent times Austin Clarke, and in turn Paul Durcan, are both highly regarded for their critical take on Irish society. Even with websites such as Waterford Whispers News performing a similar function, satirical poetry is surely needed today as much as ever.

Kevin Higgins' *Song of Songs 2.0: New and Selected Poems* demonstrates the full range of his deadpan humour and cutting parodies. He is at home in the post-modern world, and moves easily through his bewildering cast of characters and concerns. Taking a quick glance through the new poems collected here, one sees references to Trotsky, General Pinochet, Bruce Forsyth, Gary Glitter, Mitt Romney, Genghis Khan, Jimmy Saville, and Kate Bush. Topics for his satire include mindfulness, celebrity cooks, Enda Kenny, and often Higgins himself. This is a world that the internet has made possible, where we are accustomed to shifting between vastly different subjects at the touch of a keyboard button. Higgins' poetry engages with this world, making fun of it but with the full intention of making serious points.

The opening poems of the collection are new, and the first three mock the poet himself as he notes the ravages of time and the roads not taken. In 'To Those Who Preferred The Old Kevin', for example, he apologises for the sort of changes many suffer as they move from the idealistic 'boy who loved / Nicaraguan peasants / and striking coalminers' to a world-weary reality. In many ways this poem, like all Higgins' best work, is a political poem, as it deals with life in an increasingly cynical world. Higgins grew up in London and Galway, and was politically active from the 1980s, opposing the poll-tax in the early nineties when he was based in England. Those years were a time when politics still mattered deeply, and the gulf between the Thatcherite right-wing and the old Labour Party was huge. In this poem Higgins is implying that not only is the young Higgins no more, but those left-wing values have faded too:

> Tomorrow I'll send you
> a ring of white lilies
>   and my sympathy
> on the death of who
>   the fool I was
> made you think you were.

Higgins is currently suspended from the British Labour Party for writing a satirical poem about Tony and Cherie Blair, proving that poetry does still matter and that the pen does still wield some power to unnerve and discomfort the political class. The case has been a minor *cause célèbre* with Higgins receiving support from fellow writers and activists, including notable figures such as Ken Loach. It is odd that a reworking of Bertolt Brecht's 'Ballad of the Soldier's Wife' should cause offence, particularly since Blair has been the subject of war crimes accusations ever since the Iraq war. Quite rightly, Higgins' new work continues to rail against the hypocrisies of contemporary politics, setting his sights on a broad spectrum of elected representatives in several countries – from the election of 'Donald J. Duck' in the United States to a poem about tax after Michael Noonan.

The satire in Higgins' work is not restricted to politics; as one reads through the new poems to the selections from previous collections, the reader is drawn into a slightly askew version of the world the rest of us inhabit. His vision slips into an absurdist alternate reality akin to some of the poetry written in Eastern Europe during the Cold War. In fact, as Philip Coleman points out in his 'Afterword' to this collection, the Albanian poet Visar Zhiti has also been an acknowledged influence. There are also a couple of poems here after Dennis O'Driscoll, himself a writer influenced by a number of Eastern European poets, and some re-writing of classic songs; Kate Bush's 'Wuthering Heights' becomes 'Laddering Tights', and Gil Scott-Heron's 'The Revolution Will Not Be Televised' turns into 'The New Rising Will Not Be Available Later On The RTÉ iPlayer'. The jokes don't always work, however, and Higgins' rewriting of 'Do They Know It's Christmas?' seems uncharacteristically flat.

Nevertheless, there is so much going on in this collection that it is like entering an idiosyncratic microcosm of the twenty-first century. When the satire hits home it can be deliciously satisfying. In 'Conference Speech', for example, he captures the tone and style of the British Party Conference to perfection, satirising here the deadpan dull delivery of Theresa May and the middle England she represents:

Who am I? And what on earth am I doing here?
Let me be clear. Each time I stand up to speak
as your Prime Minister, the church organist at Midsomer
kills again:

It is this ability to wring the ridiculous out of the sopping clothes of everyday life that makes Higgins' work essential reading. *Song of Songs 2.0: New and Selected Poems* is the ideal introduction to his world and, by extension, ours too.

Eamonn Wall is probably less known in Ireland than Higgins despite having published six previous collections of poetry with Salmon. He is from Co Wexford originally, but has lived in the United States since 1982, where he is currently a professor of Irish Studies and English at the University of Missouri-St. Louis. Wall's writing often bridges the Atlantic, with references to Ireland and Wexford in particular stitched into the more dominant presence of America and American literature.

The title poem, 'Junction City', sets out a major theme for this collection, that of finding one's place in the world. Here, one's early morning breath is 'Expelled', as though forced out reluctantly into the air. And even while on a bus in Kansas the poet's thoughts are never far from the Irish Sea and a flash of light from a jet-ski there. Back in the aptly named Junction City, Wall notes that 'the road you travel / and the road you dream merge', the junction then is one between the imagination and reality. Place becomes a meeting point for ideas and experiences with the poet concluding:

Don't you know your place?
My home is where I am, old wise blue bus.

For an Irish poet living in America the thoughts of immigration are never far away, and several of Wall's poems refer to it directly. The poem 'Immigrants', for example, is a harshly realist depiction of the loneliness of the displaced: 'Our doors are bolted to America. / Our dreams fastened to no promised land.' In a longer piece, 'The Wexford Container Tragedy 2001', Wall traces links between historical immigration and more recent events and tragedies. One section of this 'tidy narrative' deals with the deaths of eight Kurdish stowaways travelling to Ireland to what they thought would be a better life. The poem also details a visit to the New York Holocaust Museum and to Ellis Island, where the poet is again drawn to thoughts of Wexford and the realisation:

How quickly for each immigrant all can fall apart
in fits of panic and dismay.

Movingly, the dead Kurds become – in the last section of the poem – native to Wexford, as nationality is subsumed by common suffering and the search for 'promised / employment, if not salvation'. They have become a part of the local history, but 'Our Wexford people / would never eat our strawberries, drink our tea'.

Despite all the references made to Ireland, Wall's poetry seems to fit more snugly into the American tradition. The poems are written largely in unrhymed free verse, and they roll along confidently from place to place. There are several prose poems, and Wall's reading is clearly indebted to writers such as Anne Carson, Lawrence Ferlinghetti, and Hart Crane, who are all mentioned or acknowledged. Wall's embracing of America has meant that although he is nostalgic for Ireland, he also realises that the times have moved on. In a poem 'For the Gathering', written about the 2013 initiative to encourage those with Irish roots to visit the country, Wall says, 'we know it is impossible to collar / Shoals rendered so long invisible'. This *New and Selected Poems* covers poems from 1990 to 2015, and shows a poet writing convincingly about some of the major issues of our times.

Catherine Ann Cullen is a native of Drogheda, and has published two full collections of poetry, along with verse-stories for children, before *The Other Now*. She is a graduate of the M.Phil in Creative Writing at Trinity College Dublin, and was writer in residence at St Joseph's School, East Wall, Dublin. This new publication collects a generous helping of previous work as well as some new poems. Her earlier collections were published by Doghouse Books, Noel King's hard-working publishing house, which sadly ceased producing new work in 2013.

Memory and childhood loom large in these poems, as minor remembered events take on a wider significance. In the title poem, a child takes two sweets, eating one immediately and saving the second for 'the other now'. This poem captures the simplicity of a moment and yet notes how it resounds through other presents, all our experiences interconnected. In 'Introvert', the poet is able to turn time on its head by running a film backwards, so that a pebble thrown into water 'leaps back to my fingers'. The pebble is then inextricably linked to the poet herself who becomes 'a dark stone / that makes no splash'.

One of the most impressive pieces of work here is the poetic sequence entitled 'Seven Works of Mercy', based around the Caravaggio work of the same name situated in the church of Pio Monte della Misericordia in Naples. Each of the seven sections of the poem refers to one of the works of mercy depicted in the painting. In the first section, 'Miracle in Naples – Feeding the Hungry', Cullen recalls visiting the chapel just as the security guard is closing up: 'We beg for one taste of our summer's last Caravaggio'. Cullen skilfully shifts perspective throughout the sequence, moving effortlessly into the minds of the characters in the painting as well as to the painter himself, 'the master of tricks of light'. Caravaggio's work was shocking for its honest portrayal of the seedier side of Italy in the late sixteenth and early seventeenth centuries. Cullen is aware of the duality in existence here, the irony of a man on the run for murder being asked 'to paint / the seven works of mercy / for the church of the incurable?' This issue is further developed in the final section, 'Virgin – Burying the Dead', and in the following stanza in particular:

> Today, at least,
> I am framed by wings.
> I'm used to a gilt halo,
> a coronet of stars,
> at least a thread of light about my hair
> but here my head is bare.

In an essay on the Dedalus Press website, Cullen writes on the importance of music for her poetry. She writes and performs her own songs, and traditional music is an important part of her family background. One can see this influence in the rhymes and rhythms of her verse and also in her use of form, not just of ballads but sonnets, sestets, and villanelles too. In 'The Ballad of Síle Na Gig' she writes a modern-day humorous and bawdy poem, with lines such as, 'it starts like a waltz and it ends like a jig, / the dance that you'll dance with a Síle na Gig'. The sexuality here is replicated in the sensuousness of other poems such as 'Oyster Girl', where 'We'd let each other's strangeness in / To harden slowly into pearls'.

The Other Now should serve to bring Cullen's work deservedly to a wider audience. While she is particularly adept at the sonnet, she appears equally comfortable using other forms. In memories and in songs, Cullen sees a way in which the past can inform the present, as she makes clear in 'In Memory of Frank Harte':

> Dublin made him and he in turn
> Built his city out of old songs,
> Resurrected heroes, restored lost bridges
> So the ghosts could cross back to us.

Peter Sirr

THE MEADOW

Where is it, the poem in which
we walk across a meadow lit
by soul light, afterglow, the burn
of recognition spreading

from corner to corner,
edge to edge as we ache
towards, infinitely towards,
not quite believing our eyes,

not quite trusting the grasses,
hardly daring to breathe
the air in which we both
too late appear, one of us

raising a hand, one of us opening
the conversation in which
everything is forgiven, everything
forgotten, where is it, that one?

Amy Gaffney

IN A PICKLE OF A PLACE

Behind us, down the cushioned mountainside,
The copper branched hedges gleam in buttermilk light,
In the fields, the stubble stabs at our boots, and stretches pointy
    fingers up the way.
Our jeans snag on brambles
As we search for the place where we will indulge in tea and tin-foil
    wrapped cheese rolls.

Each mouthful crisp,
Pickle spiced.

Each sip heaven,
Artificial sweeteners,
For me.
Sugar for you.

The boulder juts from the gorse's spiny grasp,
A bride in a holy veil of gossamer lace, dream spun.
A kitchen.
An altar.
Sacrifices have been made here.

It's the perfect place for a pickled piece.

No phone signal. No getting away
From
Difficult conversation.

No one can see us.
We can see no one;
But each other.

Mairéad Byrne

COCKS

In Casarabonela the cocks don't agree on who's boss
so each, occupying his own orbit like a plinth, crows.
They all get daybreak right even when the sun,
sequestered in the mist, doesn't show,
fulminating in the Green Room, and the sky's
an uncompromising curtain, all the bigger for being grey,
billowed with the traces of its lowering, and in places
moving like smoke or intensifying
as if a lamp behind it's burning.

They crow at other times too, when a motor cycle
struggles up the perpendicular
streets of the pueblo, hanging like an animal
from its fur, at the fanfare of the gas van,
or even sudden silence, and
sometimes they crow together,
like wolves.

The blue-green hill, out there, all material,
smoulders in its silhouette, intent on overspilling
the silver river of its incline, etched line dragging downwards
between its massing charcoal
and the waterlogged sky,

with a lone tree marching upwards –
dusky emu, shaky elephant –
marching but not moving
towards the crenellation at the top

or a mosquito feeding –
heavy-headed, feather-legged
on the line extending downwards,
arm, hand and open palm
tendering a field
of undefended skin.

Paco says *This boat is sinking and Europe is falling apart.*
I think, *Not only Europe.* And, as a corrective,
Maybe our *boat.*
                  Stung by the deaths of people
younger than ourselves, he says
Today has been a tough day.
And this time I reply –
                  Although we had no next,
old friend, I knew you when I was a child.
We hold the line so briefly.
Just now we're the people
our parents do not recognize.

Owen Gallagher

THE SADDEST PASSING
– In memory of Francis Fox, Ballinamore, Leitrim

I can see the shaft of Grandfather's cart piercing
his chest. Not in a field in Leitrim but in a street
in Glasgow. I can hear him gasp and grasp
the last of the strength he had as he stumbled
and crawled up the stairs of the tenement
to the flat where Grandmother had laid the table
and with a last tap at the door, faint as his heart,
he fell back into fearing he would never again
lay eyes on his greatest love. The door opened
and when he saw her, he sighed and sank
into the light and felt his head being lifted
and placed in her lap and he smiled when
she rubbed his hand as if trying to bring him back.
And it was enough to be held and to go like that.

Liam O'Neill

THERE IS NOTHING OF ME HERE

All-day drive to drive home.
From compass west to
encompass east; the wilds
of rock and bogland giving
way to lush and level fields.
It's a journey back the years
too, to the day I left home;
a place that is no longer
home, for me, but a place,
at most – a ghost familiar.

I look to the sky as I drive;
mute swans flying in a line,
move with haste and
purpose, returning the way
I came, as if knowing
something, but too far
removed and tongue-tied
to tell. They are escaping
something, I cannot,
for the life of me, comprehend.

This road will become my route
to all future family funerals
and I will drive then, as now,
in a dark suit, black tie with
my pale knuckles tight on the wheel.
To drive and drive again, to watch
for bends, stray cattle and swans,
until finally, and eventually,
there is nothing of me here,
that waits for my return.

Jade Murphy

PAINT

Paint on your best face with colours girl. Grief's a good canvas.
You are bright and airy. You are wholly sweet.
Sweet like French fancies and flat seven-up and sweet like toothaches in the night.
Nothing is sweeter than toothaches in the night, and
You are fresh faced. Gleaming. Like a Christmas scented tea light, or peppermint tea.
All tea. T is for terrific. T is for tremendous.
T for today and t for tomorrow and for the day after that and the day after that.
You are what's north and what's south and what's east and west.
You find your own colours to make your own rainbow.
You believe to see and see to believe and you are
Real.
Real things like love and hurt and laughing so hard your lungs bruise.
Real things like sunburn and damp towels and whistling through blades of grass.
Real things like oversleeping and overeating,
And blowing up too many balloons and passing out.
You are the most of everything. A dictionary of superlatives.
You are tall without practicing yoga, without going to church or without any heels.
You feel
Soft like tiny bunnies. Smooth like silky ribbons. Light like receipt paper.
You *ping* like a metal fork and smell like nutty granola. Blueberry muffins. Coffee
   beans. The sea.
You see wind and tears and dust.
And you hear blood flickering in your ears as you lay your head down.
Go pour yourself a glass of cranberry juice. It's morning time.
The sky is not blue but it's there.
You are fine fine fine.

Ailbhe McDaid

'LAYING HOLY MILES BETWEEN MYSELF AND HOME': SARA BERKELEY'S ECOPOETICS

> The following extract is from 'Alternative Cartographies', Chapter 2 of
> *The Poetics of Migration in Contemporary Irish Poetry,* by Ailbhe McDaid

Given the distance in both miles and years from Ireland, Sara Berkeley's collections *Strawberry Thief* (2005), *The View from Here* (2010) and *What Just Happened* (2015) are understandably neutral when it comes to expressions of national or cultural affiliation.[25] This ambivalence can be seen, however, to stretch back to her earliest work, *Penn* (1986) and *Home Movie Nights* (1989).[26] As Kathleen McCracken observes in her 1989 review, 'Berkeley's work charts conscious and unconscious territories, but what is surprising is that these landscapes rarely correspond to her native Ireland [...] The intention is neither to probe nor define a cultural identity.'[27] Berkeley's poetry is concerned with the characteristics of the landscape rather than with the inhabitants, and ecological and environmental concerns particularly underpin her later volumes. In veering away from identifiably Irish poetic concerns, Berkeley distances herself from the national literary tradition. When familiar motifs such as place, heritage, memory and loss do appear, her poems push away from collective expression, using instead a determinedly individual voice. Her engagement with the landscape is less influenced by *dinnseanchas* than by ecopoetics, and her interest is in bodies of water rather than the history of the land. In this manner, Berkeley re-envisions the landscape of poetry through her retrieval of alternate and ecocentric poetics.

The possibilities of water offer a means of circumnavigating the masculine topographical tradition of poetry rooted in Ireland. By diverging from the established norm in various ways (gender, location, subject) – and engaging a metaphor of water rather than earth – poetic and thematic spaces are opened out in which diverse experiences may be positioned. The element of water is manifestly appropriate for female migrant poets in America, not least for its resistance to the grounding affect of traditional

---

25 Sara Berkeley, *Strawberry Thief* (Co. Meath: The Gallery Press, 2005); *The View from Here* (Co. Meath: The Gallery Press, 2010); *What Just Happened* (Co. Meath: The Gallery Press, 2015).
26 Sara Berkeley, *Penn* (Dublin: Raven Arts Press, 1986); *Home Movie Nights* (Dublin: Raven Arts Press, 1989); *Facts About Water: New and Selected Poems* (Dublin: New Island Books, 1994).
27 Kathleen McCracken, 'Review of Home Movie Nights and Penn,' *The Canadian Journal of Irish Studies* 15, no. 2 (1989).

Irish poetry.[28] Its inherently feminine principles of fertility and fluidity propose alternative modes of engagement, while the significance of water to the migrant consciousness retains its historical relevance. The trans-atlantic journey has defined the flow of emigrant traffic to the United States for generations and even in the era of easy air travel, the symbolic significance of crossing the ocean retains its power.

While the Atlantic separates, it also connects the two shores and water is the binding element that links the land-masses. The mutability of water means its shape is defined by its boundaries: shorelines form outlines and coasts offer contours to an otherwise amorphous element. Similar to the ways migrants are bound to drift between home- and host-lands, the fluctuations of water are measured by its interactions with local terrain. The cultural, social, historical and communal characteris-tics of the land define and dictate the migrant's relationship to the new society as well marking his/her negotiations with the place left behind. Oceans and seas have a particular significance in the divided migrant consciousness, but other bodies of water are also meaningful, especially in a contemporary suburban American context. The image of the lake as a pleasure-place, a site of retreat and recuperation, reaches back to Thoreau's *Walden* (1854), offering immersion in an all-American existence. Its symbolic function as a repository of time and history is problematised by the lake's stagnant passivity, however. Rivers, on the other hand, are linear progressions through time, space and place, and propose another series of symbolic significances for female poets moving beyond existing paradigms. Berkeley's ethic of reinvention rejects limiting topographical memory frames and instead recovers alternative sites of memory in which she situates her poetry.

Through the mediated prism of photographic memory, Berkeley intimates the appropriated nature of her central imagery. Black and white photographs frame Berkeley's volume *The View from Here*, acting as imagistic prompts that participate in the collection's remembering of the social significance of water-scapes while also inveigling themselves into the reader's cognitive memory of reading the volume. The opening im-age captures a small jetty on a still lake, with distant houses reflected in the water's surface, while the final image shows a rusty boathouse on the shoreline, with its jetty stretching into water that fades, borderless, into the white of the page. In bookending the volume with visual reminders of its central element, Berkeley nods to the structural and thematic im-portance of water in *The View from Here*. Whether in man-made or natural bodies, water figures throughout; indeed she goes so far as to confess her infatuation in 'Swimming Pool':

---

28 See Gerardine Meaney, 'History Gasps: Myth in Contemporary Irish Women's Poetry,' in *Poetry in Contemporary Irish Literature* ed. Michael Kenneally (Buckinghamshire: Colin Smythe, 1995) for discussion of water and myth in poetry by Irish women writers, including references to Berkeley's earlier collections.

I have fallen for water,
a silky bolt of it, rolling and unrolling
under the heavy sky.

THE VIEW FROM HERE, 20.

The banality of the suburban pool-side setting is transformed into a scene of mythic import, charged with power and profundity. The poet sees her 'kneeling by the water, / a makeshift altar', in an offering of the self. The elemental purity of water heals as, in harmony with the sun and the trees, it 'breaks life down to its simplest concerns'. The setting invokes a Mediterranean location with the 'sun slanting through the olive tree'. The final verse transforms the girl into Persephone.

If I did not have her
there would be no more summer
and the darkness would not go
with the night.

THE VIEW FROM HERE, 20.

If Persephone is the daughter-figure, then the poet is Demeter, and this is surely a conscious allusion, considering the poet's environmental and ecological concerns. Elsewhere, in 'Carrying', Persephone reappears 'among the wild iris and the blue-eyed grass; / she filled her basket, she was overflowing', while Demeter engages her archetypal emotions, coming to understand her 'own mother's sleepless nights / and the fury of her love'. The retrieval of the Persephone myth here surely owes a debt to Eavan Boland's 'The Pomegranate' as well as to inherited versions of the Greek and Roman stories.

As an allusion, Berkeley's remembering and reinvention of Boland's poem operates on multiple levels of memory. 'The Pomegranate' is a poem of motherhood, of loss and of inevitability.[29] It is also itself an act of repudiation – the poem refuses to remember Cathleen Ní Houlihan as the female archetype in poems of mythology within the Irish tradition. Boland's retrieval of memory that lies outside the parameters of Irish myth is central to her ethic of reinvention, as asserted in both her prose writing and within her poetry itself.[30] The enabling influence of Boland's poetics for subsequent generations of Irish women poets is harnessed in Berkeley's poetry, which retains Boland's memory practices, not only in

---

29 Eavan Boland, *New Collected Poems* (New York: Norton, 2008).
30 Eavan Boland, *Object Lessons: The Life of the Woman and the Poet in Our Time* (New York: Norton, 1995). See also Kerry E. Robertson, 'Anxiety, Influence, Tradition and Subversion in the Poetry of Eavan Boland,' *Colby Quarterly* 30, no. 4, December (1994); Anne Fogarty, ' "The Influence of Absences": Eavan Boland and the Silenced History of Irish Women's Poetry,' *Colby Quarterly* 35, no. 4, December (1999).

its mythic principles but also in the way the younger poet engages intergenerational anxieties along expressly female lines.

The complex, evolving dynamics between mother and daughter preoccupies a number of poems, as reflected in this deceptively harmonious couplet from 'Carrying', a title that services the weighty reciprocity of the relationship:

> we carry our daughters until they are too light to bear,
> then we carry our mothers; they are heavy as air.
>
> THE VIEW FROM HERE, 16.

Berkeley's personal journey of motherhood occupies her poetic thought, with poems marvelling at the wonder of her growing child. In 'Approaching Eight', the balance of independence and need, of individuality and inheritance embodied in the young girl, enchants the poet.

> I never thought
> eight would be so fragile,
> so delicate, so robust, such a synthesis,
> a symphony, a gallery full
> of astonishing art. For my part,
> now and then,
> I see where I held the brush.
>
> THE VIEW FROM HERE, 23.

The daughter is a precious creation but possesses a force of her own, a force that is almost otherworldly at times, one whom 'the fairies number [...] among their own'. Here, in 'The Business of Rain', the daughter becomes elemental in her own way, embracing the rainstorm as 'she opens the windows, / she opens all the doors; / [...] / and she bursts upon the great outdoors'. As for Eamonn Wall and his daughter, the synchronicity between the child and nature reconfigures the poetic relationship with physical and emotional landscapes. In Berkeley's poetry, it engenders reflections on the substance of nature in terms of universal human experience. The element of water dictates the lexicon of poems such as 'Dark Summer Days' and 'Approaching Eight' that transfigure the difficulties of growing up into metaphors of voyage and expedition. The daughter's books and toys become 'the bowed and weathered instruments of her navigation', her strength 'driving up like a mast through the sea foam'. The precariousness of life's journeys, even at this early stage, is pronounced.

In fragile possession of her course
and her own short set of ship's orders
she steps bravely out with me onto the burning waters.

THE VIEW FROM HERE, 19.

The lure of the water, despite its dangers, is perceptible to both poet and daughter, who knows 'how scary, / that moment when the oar / rode up, what a relief / to make it back to shore, / how tomorrow you want more'. The solo journey on the water is a kind of rite of passage, and Odyssean trip across the ocean with dangers lurking beneath the surface. The ocean's charm seduces the poet in 'Heart's Desire', tempting her to relinquish her worldly worries through immersion.

She rocked me back and forth
with the small swell of occasional boats
and I sank my head into her muffled reedy world.

THE VIEW FROM HERE, 22.

For Berkeley, water tantalises with offers of escape – declaring 'all roads lead to the sea' – while remaining elusively untameable and unattainable: 'they don't belong to me, the snatches / of blue sea between the winded trees'. Steering a way through unfamiliar spaces defines Berkeley's journeys in poetry, and 'the bowed and weathered tools of ... navigation' chart a course that is unfailingly precarious. 'Azimuth' considers the urge for exploration, its title a technical term principally used in navigation or astronomy. An azimuth is the measure of the angle of the horizon's arc and, as well as establishing a motif of charting routes, the title also continues the undercurrent of nautical references, emphasising the poem's central theme that draws on, and ultimately dismisses, man-made land maps. Like the titular parallax of Sinéad Morrissey's 2014 collection, the angle of the azimuth is dependent on the position and perspective of the observer. By centring subjectivity through mathematical and astronomical concepts, Berkeley imposes a deliberate stamp of individuality that rejects any implication of articulations along collective or national lines.

The distrust in hegemony is extended by again invoking the senior female poet Eavan Boland; her poem 'That the Science of Cartography is Limited' is referenced through Berkeley's depiction of the unreliability of plotted demarcations on the page.[31] The stasis of sketched lines is anathema to the changing scapes of the migrant's journey: 'I am going on alone / through towns redrawn since we were young.' In this *unheimlich* place, maps prove no guide. But where Boland seeks the stories hidden between contours, Berkeley refuses the atlas entirely. 'We are much farther north

---

31 Boland, *New Collected Poems.*

than we ever meant to be' the poem confesses, a statement that reveals the folly of following the map as well as a deeper conviction of not belonging. The poem resorts instead to the body, to nature and to the vocabulary of water as trustworthy alternative coordinates. The mutability of maps in 'Azimuth' reinforces Berkeley's belief in the fundamental flux at the heart of human experience that is best expressed through fluid metaphors of water.

> On my hands river veins, maps of the years,
> hands that anointed you with oils,
> sandalwood, jojoba, lavender for rest.
>
> *THE VIEW FROM HERE*, 34.

The narrator's confidence in the lines of her hands, and the easy synchronicity between water and body, contrasts sharply with the ensuing stanza's difficulty in articulating the inner life.

> But how to express — I need my mother tongue
> for this — *l'étrangeté* — strangeness of the ghost
> who walks alone inside my shoes.
>
> *THE VIEW FROM HERE*, 34.

The formal stutter brought about by the caesurae echoes the emotional content of the difficult lines, lines that reach for another language to express themselves. The 'strangeness of the ghost' draws on ideas of the *unheimlich* and the foreigner, which refract Berkeley's personal experience as an emigrant. The multiple selves of the exilic subject can't help but engender psychic crises of identity, suggested here in linguistic inadequacy and expressive limitations. Personal and cultural alienations are tightly woven, and the paradoxical urge for familiarity as well as distance is expressed towards the end of the poem: 'I ride the same train every afternoon / laying holy miles between myself and home.'

The sense of the uncanny infusing the poet's observations defines her relationship to these foreign places. Peculiarities in nature are eerie and foreboding, at times threatening to disrupt the natural order as she understands it. 'There are bees at the flowers in December. It is not right / to live like this down here in the half-light.' These disturbances are distressing to her instincts, an affront to her understanding of how the world works. Berkeley's expectations are challenged by this foreign climate, and she perceives a catastrophic aspect to these natural digressions, anticipating the deluge. '[I]t's never rained like this before / at Easter. Where the colours should be pale yellow, pale blue, they are an unremitting slate'. This tarnished land is an alien place, full of suffering and distress. The strangeness she perceives is, on one level, borne out of her outsider status but the poet is equally concerned with the profound damage to 'the robbed earth' that translates across cultures and countries. Berkeley's ecopoetic approach equates the environmental and seasonal disruption with insidious ecological and social devastation. 'Absolution' develops those connections between personal and public crises, indicting both herself and society.

> I'm at the low-water mark
> and I want the journey back.
> I sold it, or someone stole it,
> and now those same little birds
> with the bleeding throats
> can hardly sing their way past
> the dark stain of hunger, the loneliness.
>
> *THE VIEW FROM HERE, 63.*

The limitations of birdsong are also the limitations of poetry, for 'there aren't even / adequate words for it / down here in the wreckage'. Post-apocalyptic images invade Berkeley's poetic view of 'the parched earth'. Reflections on endings and deaths, on how 'the flowers starved / the streams ran dry', and the sound of the wind which 'rolled through the cottonwoods / like labour pains', are scattered throughout her work, even in poems espousing hope.

In its title, 'Absolution' points to the possibility of pardon and its final lines are an act of faith in 'the world turning constantly from depletion / towards forgiveness, absolution'. Berkeley offers a prayer for release that is Beckettian in its recognition of the cyclical stasis of existence: 'I want to come to the end / of coming to the end, begin again / as though there had never been / that sparse, underfed exhaustion.' These lines, and the poem's earlier invocation of birdsong, water and spring, also call forth Brendan Kennelly's poem 'Begin' with its opening encouragement to '[b]egin again to the summoning birds / to the sight of light at the window'.[32]

Aspirations of fresh starts are linked to prospects of escape in Berkeley's aesthetic. The suggestion of incarceration brought about by the poet's prayers for release is accentuated by multiple mentions of exits and escape routes. The possibilities of water resurface in 'A Thousand Letters' where 'all roads lead to the sea', whereas '59th Street Bridge' proposes alternate methods while stressing that 'the time for flight has come'. With 'escape routes inked on our palms', Berkeley is urgent in her need to break away from this uncanny place which is both utterly strange yet

---

32 Brendan Kennelly, *The Essential Brendan Kennelly* (North Carolina: Wake Forest University Press, 2011).

troublingly familiar.

> It isn't mine, the grey road
> that wanders on down to the point
> [...]
> They don't belong to me, the snatches
> of blue sea between the winded trees,
> the painful greens, so like home,
> the milk trucks lumbering by with their payload.

THE VIEW FROM HERE, 28.

Wes Davis proposes that Berkeley's 'poems of memory and loss link her to a longer poetic tradition than first glance might suggest', and this can also be perceived in the bereft quality to her writing.[33] An awareness of the past and its extinct possibilities enthrals Berkeley, as she ventures back to junctions to lament what might have been lost. 'I wish I had built more fences, taken down more fences' she keens in 'Meals for Friends', a poem that laments and rejoices life in equal measure. Like the *Cailleach Beara*, the speaker rues the onset of old age while acknowledging the joys of her life. 'Everything I needed to remember / has been remembered; everything I yearned to forget / is lost.' Trust in the natural order trumps human expectation, hopes revealed as foolish when 'the ocean gives its undivided attention'. Yet for all the nonchalance, the final line suggests the vulnerability of the human condition and offers little consolation as the last reflections of an aged narrator in asking 'what matter now / when the heart has proved such a porous vessel for love?'

The presentation of fragmented and devastated individual lives highlights the ecopoetic impetus behind Berkeley's poetry. Along with a heightened sense of the uncanny, this disorder permeates Berkeley's perception of the natural world, an awareness intensified by her migrant status as well as by her eco-consciousness. At the core of Berkeley's poetry is a post-pastoral aesthetic that sees human culpability in the devastation of the earth's natural resources. Through this lens, the significance of water in her writing is more than a poetic device of self-liberation from migration and national narratives; the post-pastoral speaks out of an ethic of responsibility to larger environmental and ecological concerns. While the traditional pastoral mode, especially in the Irish tradition, uses nature as a means of redeeming history or violence, or as a unifying tribal motif, Berkeley's poetry refuses distinctions between nature and culture, treating both as a single integrated system. Historically the pastoral is concerned with landscape, countryside (in opposition to city) and idealisation; the specifics of post-pastoral ethics differ in kind. Arguments have been made

---

33 Wes Davis, ed. *An Anthology of Modern Irish Poetry* (Harvard: Harvard University Press, 2010): p. 858.

for (and against) the consideration of prominent Irish poets, including Heaney, Longley and Murphy, as writing in an ecopoetic or/and post-pastoral mode.[34] It is worth noting also the emergence of ecofeminist criticism that considers post-pastoral traits in a gendered context, especially in Adrienne Rich's poetry; this approach is particularly illuminating with regard to the work of Moya Cannon, Medbh McGuckian and Mary O'Malley, as analysed by Donna L Potts and James McElroy.[35] Ecofeminism provides another interpretive dimension to Berkeley's work although this analysis is less concerned with gender than with post-pastoral elements in her writing. A post-pastoral approach allows contemporary migratory poetry to move beyond 'a preoccupation with place as an unseverable aspect of self' to address universal environmental issues which Berkeley views with ethical and poetical urgency.[36]

Thanks to Palgrave Macmillan and to Ailbhe McDaid for their permission to include this excerpt from *The Poetics of Migration in Contemporary Irish Poetry* (Palgrave Macmillan, 2017).

For more information about this book, see www.palgrave.com/la/book/9783319638041.

---

34 Oona Frawley, *Irish Pastoral: Nostalgia and Twentieth-Century Irish Literature* (Dublin: Irish Academic Press, 2005); Edna Longley, 'Pastoral Theologies,' in *Poetry and Posterity*, ed. Edna Longley (Newcastle-upon-Tyne: Bloodaxe Books, 2000); Donna L. Potts, *Contemporary Irish Poetry and the Pastoral Tradition* (Columbia, Missouri: University of Missouri Press, 2011); Christine Cusick, *Out of the Earth: Ecocritical Readings of Irish Texts*, (Cork: Cork University Press, 2010); Eamonn Wall, 'Wings beating on stone: Richard Murphy's ecology,' in *Out of the Earth: Ecocritical Readings of Irish Texts*, ed. Christien Cusick (Cork: Cork University Press: 2010).
35 James McElroy, 'Ecocriticism and Irish poetry: a preliminary outline,' *Estudios Irlandeses* 6, no. (2011).
36 John Wilson Foster, 'The Geography of Irish Fiction,' in *Colonial Consequences*, ed. John Wilson Foster (Dublin: Lilliput Press, 1991).

Lucy Collins

ALTERNATIVE CARTOGRAPHIES

Ailbhe McDaid, *The Poetics of Migration in Contemporary Irish Poetry*
(Palgrave Macmillan, 2017), €103.99 hb.

Migration is among the most pressing of contemporary political issues,
challenging the concept of national identity and presenting urgent moral
dilemmas. In the Irish context, periods of intense emigration have recently
given way to patterns of intermittent immigration, and to the ensuing
emergence of new communities. Brian Lenihan's assertion, in the late
1980s, that 'we can't all live on a small island' has new meaning in this
era of Direct Provision, and its prolonged injustices. In this context new
critical work on the subject of migration is much to be welcomed. This
particular study is not concerned with the experiences of those born outside Ireland, however, but rather with those born on the island who have
lived elsewhere, and who write from that displaced perspective. In this it
distinguishes appropriately between 'voluntary, emancipatory, and tem-
porary' experiences and the 'forced, traumatic and permanent' migrations
of earlier Irish history. This thoughtful and elegantly written study draws its
strengths from the acknowledged importance of Irish migrant history, but
also from its willingness to problematize received views of this experience.
It explores the work of twelve poets writing from the 1980s onwards;
most still live abroad, but some have close ties with Ireland, and have
returned to settle there, at least for a time. It is both rigorous and engaging in its treatment of individual texts, and illuminating of some important trends in current literary scholarship.

The breadth of coverage here is impressive, and at once highlights the
shared experience of these poets and the individuality of their art. Different
generations are contrasted, and attention is drawn to the varied situations of the migrant Irish – from those who moved to English-speaking
countries, such as America and Britain, and those travelling and living in
Africa, Asia, and Eastern Europe. The work of individual poets is analysed
in discrete sections gathered under larger conceptual headings, an
arrangement that allows extended engagement with the work of a single
writer while suggesting fruitful connections among these texts. More
could be made of these constellations, though: extended comparative
work would enrich the study and allow its insights to resonate in a wider
cultural context. Likewise, in representing the many ways in which
migrant experience inflects individual creativity, specific issues – such as
the relationship between migration and economic instability – remain
under-examined. In this respect, further attention to the role of inward

migration would enhance this work considerably. The presence in Ireland of a number of recently arrived poets has not only had an impact on the literary scene, but has altered the way Ireland's relationship with migration can be understood. Though the field of memory studies is not indicated in the title of the volume, it shapes its introduction in important ways, and emerges at various points throughout the narrative to deepen our engagement with individual texts. These theories affirm the importance of memory in both the experience and representation of migration, and their deployment could be both more selective and deliberate; for instance, an extended examination of trauma theory would have provided a useful frame for some of this discussion, and would also add complexity to the broader treatment of cultural memory.

The opening chapter is an important one in setting a framework of permanent migration to the United States as a significant dimension of Irish diasporic experience, and as a crucial factor in the critical reception of these poets. A diverse group is presented here – Eamonn Wall, Greg Delanty, and Paul Muldoon – and, fittingly, there is attention to the differences in style and readership. This chapter reveals diversity as a key feature, but there is more to be said about the assimilation of these figures within an American cultural landscape. In particular, the role of publishing practices in shaping critical perceptions is worth noting, especially given the different career trajectories here: Delanty is published by a range of US publishers, and by Carcanet in the UK; Wall's poetry volumes appear from Salmon Poetry in Ireland; Muldoon has ongoing relationships with three publishing houses – Faber, Wake Forest, and Gallery Press. The nuanced treatment of the materiality of Muldoon's texts offers something of a bridge to the second chapter – 'Alternative Cartographies' – that concerns Vona Groarke and Sara Berkeley, and suggests a very different perspective on American texts and environments. Here more concentrated attention to form brings a new energy to the analysis, and is closely linked to the treatment of space by both of these poets. The reading of Berkeley's ecopoetic turn is especially welcome, and the transition from her early Dublin poems is briefly, but tellingly, observed. The opening pages of this chapter explicitly address the differences between male and female migrant voices. While this distinction deserves extended treatment, the points raised here help to frame the work that follows in important ways.

Three very different poets are grouped in the next chapter: Bernard O'Donoghue, Martina Evans, and Colette Bryce. The foregrounding of memory here develops some of the issues signalled in the book's introduction, and offers useful connections among diverse texts. These poets represent ambiguous migrations, and the complexity of this perspective deepens the analysis of the work. The dynamics of disappearance and reappearance, especially in Bryce's 2005 volume, *The Full Indian Rope Trick*, shape an adroit exploration of sexuality and indicate its importance in determining the conceptualisation of home. Family dynamics are central to this discussion and the analysis of *Petrol* by Evans is especially accomplished in its handling of the liminal spaces of childhood. It is satisfying in its treatment of form too, which elsewhere in the book is given comparatively slight attention. Though it would be tempting to dwell on the confessional dimensions of Evans' work, instead McDaid presents a sophisticated reading of the capacity of poetry to address the process of remembering, rather than the substance of memory itself.

Another poet whose work elicits a particularly rich reading is Harry Clifton. The section on his work explores a process of ongoing movement that problematizes the binary aspects of singular relocation. Derek Mahon is an exemplar here, and the entwined reading of his 'Everything is Going to be Alright' and Clifton's 'Dying Generations' deepens our understanding of deracination in the work of both poets. The persistent likening of Clifton to the 'wandering Jew' does require further unpicking, though, and could offer a productive point of connection with Sinéad Morrissey's representation of the formative effects of family and ancestry. The sectarian contexts of Belfast are important to this reading of her work and could yield interesting comparisons with Bryce's treatment of her Derry childhood. The dynamics of presence and absence, of memory and forgetting, might also have been probed further in the context of civil strife, especially given that in particular communities – those of South Africa and Northern Ireland, for example – the capacity to forget is judged essential to a regenerative politics.

In choosing to end this study with the work of Justin Quinn and Conor O'Callaghan, McDaid turns to the role of technology in the formation of contemporary identity. For both these poets technology plays an important role in linking communities to capitalist structures of relation. The contrast between Quinn's approach to virtual embodiment and that earlier recorded in Groarke's poems is suggestive, and is just one example of the ways in which close readings resonate across this study. Though the divergent cultural contexts of this final pairing of poets would bear more sustained examination, the emphasis here is on the movement beyond national identification and fixed subjectivities. The combination of anonymity and intimacy that technology permits offers an effective conclusion to this thought-provoking and significant study, as well as indicating future directions for work on contemporary Irish poetry.

Kate O'Neill

AWAY WITH YOU

– for my grandfather

When young lads call on the black candlestick telephone
an Irish immigrant with four dark-haired daughters dare not say
Away with you – she's above your kind.
No, better to sound a wee bit daft or rather grand.
No, she cannot talk right now.
She's in the linen closet
giving the parrot
a bath.

Scott McKendry

GREASEPAINT

> *Because the revolutionary priests and school-masters served Man,*
> *they cut the throats of men.*
> – Saint Max, aka Max Stirner, alias Johann Kaspar Schmidt

How Carl Marks got through seven years of primary school
without a raised eyebrow, never mind sniggering, at roll call

God only knows.

Grammar school was for him however, a whole other animal
from Friday on the first week of first form, when Mr McCaw

took us off syllabus

due to a cold: "We're off-road," he said, "ask anything at all."
The swot threw up a hand and posed a question, but McCaw

drew a blank –

so he told us in detail about the Storming of the Winter Palace
and about its re-enactment, *The Storming of the Winter Palace,*

and not for the last time.

McCaw had us chanting 'Len*in*, Len*in*' when I hit Carl Marks
up the face, full pelt, with the fattest superglue-injected conker

the world has ever seen. It was

amazing. And as his sobbing swoll to a high-pitched squall,
Dipso McCaw halted the incantation with an upturned palm

and told Carl to shush.

After a few weeks and ten more colds, the name of each pupil
had sunk in. Though McCaw couldn't accept that Carl's name

was just a happen-so.

"No, no, no, no, no, no, no. No way. You mean to tell me, son,
at the very least, yur daddy's not involved with a trade union?"

During this interrogation,

Marks just shook his head and grinned. During PE, he told me
he was scared he'd end up a bitter wreck, like Paul McCartney

from the year above us,

whose mum was taken by a bout of late-onset Beatlemania.
Carl went on eBay and bought all four volumes of *Capital*

and a tube of black greasepaint.

Iain Twiddy

THE SHREDDER

Late Friday night, my department,
the usually throbbing copy room –
the strip lights, the white horizons of blinds,
the windows as blank as the ice they hide –

shredding a life like high-piled snow, evidence
of existence in this big-wintered city:
savage drafts of a gone-wrong novel,
red hackings-at, stumblings and skids into stories,

the first numbed shapings of poetry's snows,
frittering and bagging, depriving of air
the call I left home, as from Hamelin,
a decade ago alone to follow.

The shredder – mid-chew – stalls.
I crouch down, reach the length of an arm
head-tiltingly into a big back end.
I crouch there longer than I should, perhaps,

shouldering, sheltering, between the copy machines;
as if in reaching further, past the jam
in the chute, I might feel my father,
might draw him out, warm as a newborn calf.

Mark Granier

WORKSHOP

Find your personal lexicon, your best
and precious word-hoard. Make a list
of favourites – *hoard, lexicon, spindrift, drought,*
saccade, arabesque, smithereens – the kind your mouth
was shaped for: *socket, vermilion, pilfer, dross* –

Now think of the sort of characters you'd cross
the road to avoid, ones you'd curse with a grim
vocabulary – *Awesome, loser, meme,*
OMG, mansplaining, Sad! – and cheerful tips
like *wake-up-and-smell-the... read my...* Close their lips

till they swallow your medicine, this nourishing
they were born to spit out, sing.

Katie Sheehan

LIGHTCHASING
  for Niall

You leave the house bleary-eyed
and ready for work, to see the sky awash
in purple and gold. Turn heel
and tear into the labyrinth of side roads,
past uniformed huddles of children
and the sensible commuters waiting for their buses.
Through the musk of last night's fires.
Eastward. You arrive at the water's edge
where lamps glow dim in the morning
light, now grown less wild itself.
Press on anyway. Flocks of elegant Brent,
newly arrived from the north, draw low
and winding V's across the water.
Two ferries slip between the harbour walls,
and behind them the grey splits a sliver
and sun spills out in an intimate blaze,
cloaking the broken cloud in colour.
How could you have known
it was for this that you had travelled?
The star never burns so close
for the landlocked. After a time, you too
must make your way back from the shore,
toward the office and your whole waiting life.
But before you leave the promenade,
turn around just once, turn
to take one last look at her
as she makes poetry of the labouring
shipyard across the bay.
For you are no Orpheus, friend,
and she will return again tomorrow.

Attracta Fahy

ENCOUNTERS

Staring at the long queue of silent people
staring at blank wounded faces who gaze
staring past grimaced façades in lifeless bodies
staring with fear that haunts look away smiles
staring into a mauve shabby purse that's almost empty
staring back at a clouded window that reflects my age
staring down at pleated bills I'm trying to pay
staring through the aloof woman in the distance
staring at those who once were friends
staring at iPhone photos of my children
staring grateful for the rich life of my handbag

Ray Givans

DEVELOPMENT

The letter from Head Office
lies open on my desk; a blur of hieroglyphs
since I read, '… no longer required.'

They say it's like the grief that follows death.
In these three months I slip away more
and more to the darkroom. When it comes

to closing day – Christmas Eve – the shop bell
will keep on chiming. The shutters,
with their familiar guttural, will rise again, New Year.

The customers I most dislike are those who come
to gather all the info, stats, who poke a finger
into every crevice of the equipment, then scurry off

to buy online. I no longer make a play of politeness;
give them twenty minutes. "Are you here to buy or not?"
If only I had insisted on online selling. If only

I had taken on Restorations. If only…
Most days my lunchbox remains unopened.
I walk the grounds of The City Hall,

where, recently, I watched the stuttering steps
and bobbing heads of a pair of ring-necked doves
dining-out on the lawns. One day the stouter female

failed to show. For days after
the male wandered in circles, stopped
at familiar places, as if in a daze.

Light? Employers from the Ford Motor Company
called twelve of us to a local hotel,
laid out an array of tests, full of pitfalls

and slips for the unwary. Only one was chosen.
I made the final cut. Hold on to this unsteady torch.

David Butler

LISTENING FOR ECHOES

Stephanie Conn, *Island* (Doire Press, 2018), €12.
Sean Borodale, *Asylum* (Cape Poetry, 2018), £10.
Ellen Cranitch, *The Immortalist* (Templar Poetry, 2017), £10.
Adam Wyeth, *The Art of Dying* (Salmon Poetry, 2016), €12.

Poetry has a long and venerable tradition of interrogating the intersection of landscape and identity. Stephanie Conn's second collection, *Island*, expands on her award winning chapbook *Copeland's Daughter* to consider her ancestral connections to the Copeland Islands off Donaghadee, Co Down. Early in the collection, she sounds a note of warning:

> The people here had no time for sea-gods
> who shepherd seals or speak of the past or future;
> in these parts, that is better left unsaid.

A poem entitled 'On Visiting the Island of My Ancestors', now abandoned to rabbits and birds, finishes on an image of a hatching gull's egg from which 'a tiny beak emerges – opens and closes, opens again'. The final two words might be read as a manifesto. If the long-gone inhabitants who eked out a living here were constitutionally reticent, Conn is determined not only to give them voice, but to imagine the voice of the abandoned landscape itself. The poem 'I am Island' finishes:

> I cannot hear the unsaid, the departed do not speak
> but cast long shadows full of dread. I am island, lost at sea.
> Amidst the weathered headstones, I hold those I can – asleep.

As might be expected, quite a number of poems deal with the trauma of emigration, though more usually viewed, as it were, through human eyes. In 'A Sea View', which might be read as a companion piece to 'I am Island', an old woman peeling potatoes sees in her mind's eye the waves she once knew:

> Her eyes are moist
> and indistinct; the watery
> blue of a newborn glance
>
> searching for mother,
> for the womb, the warm source.

The woman thinks of the young, and how they 'always rushed // to leave; someday, they too / will be old and longing / for home'. In its tightly controlled eight lines, 'As was the Custom' details how the family would gather driftwood to light a bonfire for those emigrating, while 'The Last to Leave' closes on a haunting, quasi-mythic image of a couple departing in a boat: 'I drop the Copeland / pebbles, one by one, / and watch them sink.'

But if the past was one of stoicism in the face of hardship, it was also one of camaraderie and wild beauty. 'An Excise Man Comes Calling' shows an islander's ruse of hiding gin in a crib she is rocking while also acting as lookout for a smuggling boat, while 'Biding Time', in a scene that might have been taken from Synge, describes a woman knitting a sweater as she awaits news of her missing husband, whose sweater had a dropped stitch so that he might be identified. Conn has a fine eye, too, for the natural beauty of the location. The pale-blue eggs of the black-headed gull are 'ovoid, high glossed, and fragile as a newborn's fontanelle' ('Gull Egg Season'), the island itself 'cushion-soft and punctured by rabbit holes'. But there is also a certain doubt in the poet's appropriation of the past, expressed in poems such as 'Hidden Trails', which finishes:

> Perhaps these forgotten paths that lead to the sea
> were nothing but drains, and the footsteps
> you heard were just an echo of your own.

Sean Borodale's third collection, *Asylum*, is also an interrogation of land-scape, in this case the caves, mines, and quarries of Somerset's Mendip Hills. The imaginative spaces he sounds have much in common with Derek Mahon's 'places where a thought might grow – Peruvian mines, worked out and abandoned / to a slow clock of condensation'. As in Mahon, time in Borodale's collection operates at a geological pace, removed from human activity. Thus in the ruins of the Fussell Iron-works, Borodale explores what it is like ...

> to be alone
> with the population of collapsing drips
> as they flash apart;
> with no sight, no hearing, no shallow breath;
>
> feeling the blurs of earth, feeling the bleb grow
> swelling water full of its milky stone.

Responding to a fossil, he talks of 'Time not as we know it ... Time pressed flat in a thousand directions / the fern's delicate gap resists.' But

Borodale is reluctant to push in the direction of easy metaphor. The fossilised fern is 'A small leaf-sleeve of paper, / a message meaning nothing. / A small cough in the brittle stillness / of earth floating on rock.' Elsewhere, in a fine image, he writes of a piece of slag: 'I hold the cast of a throat, / a sort of vitreous glass made of a gulp', but is careful to qualify the comparison, in the poem's title, as 'a feeling'.

Borodale's lengthy titles frequently take the form of labels or notes from a scientific field study, as for instance: 'Measuring the Effect of Darkness on the Voice for 30 Minutes, Goatchurch Cavern'. In his subterranean world of intense sensory deprivation, such voices as there are take the form of recordings which operate almost as trapped echoes. The voice of a mining surveyor is 'a penumbra, far under the place of your parents' grave'. Echoes abound. The poem 'Shatter Cave' consists entirely of the opening stanza of 'A Small Hovel Inside the Self, Eastwater Cavern', repeated verbatim three times, intensifying the eerie darkness:

> Nothing has come here
> that is more than flicker,
> that has not brought
> the bright, hurt language of its sun.

This unusual poetic form is repeated at regular intervals throughout the collection. 'Aveline's Hole', 'Singing River Mine', and 'Sump I' in like manner consist of a stanza repeated three times, as though intensifying, in another fine image, 'the percolating leanness of light'.

As I write, Ellen Cranitch's *The Immortalist* has just been shortlisted for the Seamus Heaney Centre First Collection Prize. First collections are frequently a compilation of greatest hits over a decade or more of poetic development, and in formal terms the poems that make up *The Immortalist* are a varied bunch. If, in 'Control', 'Hellebore', 'The Suicide's Defence', 'The Graduands', and the accomplished sonnet 'The Prism', Cranitch demonstrates her aptitude for rhyme and metre, she is equally at home in the prose poem. The haunting 'The Dandelion Pit' describes the poet as she 'cradled the sunken heads, the sap, like lifeblood. I saw their souls, their odd and broken angles, learned that you can hold, in two cupped hands, the ugliness of everything you love'. The typography of 'Church Interior' mimics the subject's cruciform layout, while 'Time of Death' reworks to disturbing effect the transcript that followed the stabbing of ten year old Damilola Taylor.

Cranitch's is an enquiring, ludic mind. 'Deep Blue' imagines the machine's supposedly emotionless reaction to beating the world chess champion Gary Kasparov, suggesting that next time it might 'let him win', while '"A Tolerable Plot"', with a nod perhaps to Wallace Stevens'

'Thirteen Ways of Looking at a Blackbird', consists of thirteen meditations on the ruins of Christchurch Greyfriars, London, all beginning with
the propositional 'That …' Her poem 'Blasket Sound' neatly captures the
disorienting effect of rough seas:

> Troughs tower like something out of Exodus.
> In the pit of the wave, weighted dark,
> from which we're delivered each time to a glimpse
> of the Great Blasket, its cataclysm of gulls.

As the noun 'cataclysm' and the oxymoronic inversion 'troughs tower'
demonstrate, Cranitch's language is both controlled and inventive.
Elsewhere, she speaks of her heart's 'salmon-leap' at the sight of (of all
things!) a row of wind-turbines, 'the heart-gasp of it'.

In his second collection, *The Art of Dying*, Adam Wyeth also displays
a restless imagination in terms both of form and of tone. Wyeth is an
accomplished playwright, and the last of the three sections of this collection, 'The Hedge', has been performed as a duologue. The layout of the
poem 'Aisling', meanwhile, mimics the form of the harp that the aisling-
figure is playing – Wyeth has made studies both of the aisling form and
of references to Celtic mythology in contemporary Irish poetry. The
sequence of fifteen poems comprising the 'Talking Tree Alphabet' section, though they don't correlate directly to either the Ogham or Gaelic
tree alphabets, are undoubtedly informed by these. 'Blackthorn' incorpo-
rates the kinds of tropes extant in aisling poetry, 'Each one twisted / and
crooked like a crone', to finish with a disturbing invocation:

> …white flowers shroud
>
> her demented crown.
> Come once more my ravaged whore
> and let us kiss at the point of death.

Wyeth wears his learning lightly, and his poetry has the capacity to
amuse. 'Anatitdaephobia,' begins the poem of the same name, 'is the fear
that somewhere / in the world there is a duck watching you', 'Tomas
Transformer' plays on the name of the admired Swedish poet Tomas
Tranströmer, while 'Angry Birds' considers the 'world / of crazy kami-
kazes' of the video game of the same name. Elsewhere, in 'Fire Bird', he
talks of a flame-singed dove 'Jackson Pollocking / the walls in soot'.

But with equal facility, the poems of *The Art of Dying* can move us.
'Visiting the Poet' is an account of a hospital visit during which the
patient …

                                              ... kept wiping
his nose with a tiny section of tissue, tore off
a wet bit, folded it, then placed it in a plastic bag,

as if he was saving little parchments of life
as it leaked out of him.

The restraint of this is exemplary. In the image one can surely find a correlative for the poetic endeavour itself. Empathy is an important quality for any poet, and it is one of Wyeth's strong suits. A snatched bag witnessed in Barcelona becomes a lengthy meditation on what the victim might have lost. 'Vacuum' describes the compulsive vacuuming of a woman who has returned home from hospital 'empty-handed': 'The bag must have enough dirt, hair / and dead skin in it to form another being'. And the controlled anger underlying 'The Flesh and the Spirit' is palpable:

The night before my father died
he looked like a rabid dog
with the shit kicked out of him.

His convexed ribs poked through
the sheets, his sagging torso
a sack of rotten potatoes.

I looked down at the vandalised frame
of his life and stared into the dried-up well
of his eyes, saying his name,

waiting for an echo.

James Finnegan

THE MATHEMATICIAN IN ME

a good eye is needed to distinguish
between russet-brown and olive-green
as they are similar in size   both tiny
the latter with its yellow crown
weighing in at only five grams
        the smallest bird in Ireland
the only one smaller than the wren
    a continental goldcrest
who flew in here to Inch Levels
in late October   and whom we happened to see
on our walk around Inch Lake yesterday

    I'm not that tall myself
after a six-mile run I'm sixty-five kilograms
    thirteen thousand goldcrests
that's how small this creature is
        a life   a lifespan   a heartbeat
        how can I not care for the particular

First published in *Half-Open Door* (Eyewear Publishing, 2018)

Laura Paul Watson

SECONDARY FOREST

Love, we are two years late, crossing the strandline
of ash and lodgepole into the new leaf.
You drag the maul between us, its bit

as dull as a June bug, the sun a slurry red.
How often we took this way, stamped out
the same stories beneath the knitted August light,

and imagined ourselves unchanged, unchanging.
Remember the night we stood in the grocery store
parking lot and watched the plumes of ash

rise pink over Georgetown, the elementary school,
these same hills? Remember how we argued?
No, there is no undoing,

but around us: the slow work of forgiveness:
the sooted snag of a pine tree, and there,
a pair of juncos re-settled in the sage.

Behind us, leafless peaks,
mullein pushing up yellow and unafraid
from the cleared walls of the valley.

In these full months of summer,
they are a thousand flowered torches,
their burning buds pushing open at the tips.

Julie-Ann Rowell

ORKNEY BIRTHDAY

In the sitting room, we watch the lights go out
across the nuanced black waiting staunchly
for New Year to muscle in on her birthday.
There's no cake, no candles. She doesn't want a 'fuss'.
But the dining table is littered with surprises.
She has so many people to thank it will take weeks.
And if only Gracie would turn up her hearing aid
and Margaret didn't buy another house plant
that wants to be cared for, *noticed*.
"I don't want *anything more*," she groans.
I scan the ornaments and prints, the crystal vases,
the gilt photo frames, the sagging decorations.
What will all this stuff do without its meaning?
"Birthdays at *this* time of year," she says.

Peter Fallon

BOG COTTON

They line the banks,
a pale parade.
Ceannbhán.
Each a shade.

A gnarled
and leaning tree's
a statue cast in green
evening – and no breeze.

Then on turf scraw,
with starry bloom, by reed beds,
on scraggy stems
the seed heads

wave their downy
admonitions. Time, our rival,
ran you to ground
in those survival

acres of the corncrake.
You write from far in the west
you're lonely and you've lost
your foothold on the path to rest.

We must be open
to the world, love, in ways
that might risk
our ruin. History says

we were in each other
all along. If we could
indeed take the will
for the deed we would.

And would that I, with cotton,
could dress your spirit's cicatrix
and carry you across
each bog stream there, now River Styx.

Peter Fallon

THIS WORLD IS WORTH ITS GRIEF

Snowdrops in snow – the month's motif.
Growing light of January
suggests this world is worth its grief.

New year excoriates the thief
of all the days you'd held holy.
Snowdrops in snow – the month's motif.

The trembling hare in the last sheaf
discovers daybreak's sympathy
and learns the world is worth its grief.

Your hope to banish disbelief
renewed in new love's ministry.
Snowdrops in snow – the month's motif.

The tristful tones of *Liege and Lief*.
Believe, despite the misery
of loss, this world is worth its grief.

Resilient as the ravelled leaf
of evergreen, rail, then rally
(snowdrops in snow – the month's relief)
because this world *is* worth its grief.

Dawn Sullivan

IN THE CONSULTING ROOM

Transparently baffled, he exclaims:
"You're looking extremely glamorous!"
As if post-cancer glamour is abnormal on my part.
I could remark:
"Chipping is trivial to a work of art."
But I only smile back firmly:
"Doctor, you should say: I'm looking *well*."
And I think:
What if the professional tight-rope of our tongues
broke at both ends? And I told you how –
you'll always look extremely ugly, whether you've got
both testicles or not.

"Haven't you considered reconstruction?"
He means it *so* helpfully,
I smile and sigh:
"But Doctor *why*?
I am more preciously endowed than Venus de Milo
Can't you see? I'm embracing the world with both arms!"

He backs away; but continues:
"Body image *is* important to morale."
"Precisely Doctor, I agree;
After the real nectarine's been grown and taken
from the tree; who wants naff, stuck-on plastic fruit?"
"You seem to have slipped through,
without even being offered a prosthesis –"
"Prosthesis Doctor?
Why should *I* need a false limb more than you?
Haven't we both got hands and feet?
Doctor, I'm a woman you're talking to –
Don't confuse me with Danny La Rue!"

Cathal Ó Searcaigh

LISTENING TO THE FIRST CUCKOO CALL ON A SUNNY AFTERNOON AT THE END
OF APRIL

You rover from elsewhere
You robber, you thieving rogue
never seeing your family through to the end

But parting from them lightly
fostered on the commonage –
the meadow pipit, the robin and the dunnock.

Still, you solitary poet of the two lucid notes,
this at least to your credit
despite your questionable tendencies

That you always bring your gift
for a trusted tune and a ray of light
to cover your offences.

Didn't Blind Séamas welcome you
playfully and with a twist,
celebrating the image he would never see,

Of your slender form gentling the branches.
Didn't Wordsworth himself affirm
that your voice has the pulse of a god?

And always at this time of year
when you practise your calling
urging the music from dark to waking

I yearn for the day, I long for the hour
when the air will come to me that answers your call
and skims the film of silence from my tongue.

– translated by **David Knowles**

Translation of 'Ag Éisteacht le Céad Ghlaoch na Cuaiche Tráthnóna
Gréine i nDeireadh an Aibreáin', published in *An Bhé Ghlas* (Leabhar
Breac, 2015)

Proinsias Ó Drisceoil

PILGRIMS

Anna Frater, *Cridhe Creige* (Acair, 2017), £15.
Liam Ó Muirthile, *Camino de Santiago: Dánta, Poems, Poemas* (Cois Life, 2018), €10.

Anna Frater's only previous collection, *Fon t-Slige* (*Under the Shell*), appeared in 1995. Many poems from that book have been anthologised and are now part of Scottish Gaelic's contemporary canon; a second collection from Frater is thus a significant event. Many themes – family, community, the Gaelic language and identity – are shared by both collections, but the current volume has a more developed political character than *Fon t-Slige*: the intertwining of the public and the personal is a pervasive theme.

  Cridhe Creige (*Rock Heart*) is divided into five sections, the first and longest of which, 'Seann Phuirt' ('Old Songs') comprises linked poems from the 1990s. These are intense personal lyrics dealing with rejection, heartbreak, and the search for truth:

> B' fheàrr leam teas
> loisgeach na fìrinne
> gus am faodainn
> cuimhneachadh ort
> le blàths nam chridhe.
>   – 'CATHADH'

> I would prefer
> the burning heat of truth
> so that I could
> remember you
> with warmth in my heart.
>   – 'BLIZZARD'

Frater has always eschewed the metrically-driven aesthetic of *am bàrd baile*, the local Gaelic poet; her poems are instead markedly modernist, their pulse deriving from common speech, with the rhythms often indicated by typographical layout. Meanings are not normally made explicit: instead, multivalent narratives move towards definition in the final line or verse. Verses vary in length and the overall style is compressed, even Spartan, perhaps reflecting the austere plain-spoken Calvinism of the Isle of Lewis, where the poet was born in the village of Bayble.

  Bayble was also the birthplace of the poet, Ruaraidh MacThòmais (1921-2012), and he is undoubtedly the dominant influence on Frater's work. She shares very many of the concerns that drove MacThòmais' achievement: in particular both poets articulate in their work a strong commitment to Scottish nationalism, and her paired poems 'Ceileireadh' ('Birdsong') and 'Leòmhann Cadalach' ('Lion Dormant') are to be read as referring to Scotland before and after the failed Scottish independence referendum of 2014. In 'Ceilearadh', a linnet 'would sing for me now and then' and 'couldn't survive without me', but when it escapes the cage it goes 'singing her freedom / with happy songs'. This pre-referendum optimism meets its nadir in 'Leòmhann Cadalach'. When the lion of the poem, presumably the lion rampant of Scotland's national banner, is released from its cage:

> Chuir e a shròin a-mach.

> Agus thionndaidh e air ais.

> He stuck his nose out.

> And turned back.

The erosion of the sustaining Gaelic-speaking culture of her childhood has issued for Frater in scepticism towards the supposed benefits of Anglicised modernity with its proclaimed commitment to liberal inclusiveness. In 'Co-ionnannachd' ('Equality'), tolerance is everywhere – that is until she speaks her own language:

> Chan eil guth
> air do cho-ionnannachd
> an uairsin.

> Then
> there's no word
> of your equality.

The non-traditional forms of Gaelic now prevalent among learners of the language contrast poorly, in the poet's estimation, with the rich dialect of her native area, and in her acidic poem 'Googleamaid', she suggests that idiomatic native Gaelic is now redundant as it would only serve to complicate the work of Google Translate. Pointedly, this poem is not itself translated, presumably on the grounds that Google Translate is available to the Anglophone reader.

However, a dispirited acknowledgement of the inevitability of universal Anglicisation underlies her poem, 'Aideachadh'('Admission'):

Ach, feumar aideachadh
    nach eil na tobraichean
    às an robh mise ag òl
    anns an robh mise air mo bhogadh
      rin lorg tuilleadh.

But, I have to admit
    that the wells
    from which I drank
    in which I was immersed
      are no longer to be found.

One hopes it will not be another quarter-century before we hear this gifted voice again.

Liam Ó Muirthile ends his 2013 poem, 'Idir Dhá Fhonn Mhalla' ('Between Two Slow Airs') with a premonition:

ghabh an chomhthuiscint
ina harraing róghéar trínn
gur ghearr anois go mbeadh
an bóthar ar fad curtha dínn.

an understanding we both shared
sent shivers to the marrow
that it won't be long now
before the whole show is over
   – from *An Fuíoll Feá*, translation by Gabriel Rosenstock

By the time the volume under review came to be published, these lines had proven tragically prophetic, and Liam Ó Muirthile had completed life's pilgrimage. The collection is a short one, a mere forty-six pages, with each of sixteen poems appearing in Irish, English, Spanish, and Galician. The translations into the latter two languages are by Carmen Rodríguez Alonso; the English translations are by the author. The poems grew out of a journey along the Camino de Santiago pilgrim route which Ó Muirthile had previously described in his prose work, *Oilithreach Pinn* (Cois Life, 2017).

The poems shun personal detail but the experience of suffering is implicit throughout. The opening poem, 'An tSlí,' ('The Way'), is anxious and uncertain:

Guím
go n-éireod gach lá le fonn
tabhairt faoi,

is mura bhfuil fonn féin orm
nach ngéillfead aon lá
don lagbhrí.

I pray
that I may arise each day
to willingly walk the way,

and if I don't feel up to it
at least let me not give in
to unwillingness.

The style of the collection, as in this poem, is sparse and laconic; these are prayer-like meditations where an economy of words yields a profundity of meaning. Whereas in his previous work Ó Muirthile consciously evoked Gaelic (and French) literary influence and often played with celebrated lines from Aogán Ó Rathaille or Seán Ó Ríordáin, here he eschews such anxious influences in favour of a minimalism which sometimes allows only a word per line:

Scaob
slige
camóg
  –'MUIRÍN'

Shell
scoop
little dish.
  – 'SCALLOP'

The English translations refuse complete clarification in particular instances, as if to proclaim their own inadequacy. Thus 'camóg', while correctly given as 'little dish', has the additional meaning 'scallop shell', surely the intended meaning here, given that the scallop shell is the symbol of the Camino. Similarly, the word 'trostán' – given as 'walking stick' in the English version of the poem 'Oilithrigh' ('Pilgrims') – has the meaning 'pilgrim's staff', again the more significant meaning in the context.

    The Irish version may not, however, be the original in every instance and the book reminds one of an overlooked aspect of Ó Muirthile's genius, his ability as a writer of English, not least the elegant prose of his landmark essay, 'Offshore on Land: Poetry in Irish Now' (*A New View of the Irish Language*, 2008). Certainly, 'An Daol' ('Beetle'), one of the more full-bodied poems in the collection, might seem to flow more naturally in English than in Irish:

Theastódh an mála gaoithe gafa
ó Aeólas agus cóir lem shála
chun tabhairt faoin lá.

I would need his bag, the Keeper of Winds,
and a favourable wind from the east
at my back to face the day.

Whether this be the case or not, Irish is certainly the language of composition for 'Tocht' ('Surge'), with its elimination of all clamour and excess and its intense sense of life's worth being realised through its own journey. This is the poem in its entirety:

Tocht mochmhaidine,
ní thráfaidh go deo;
an fuíoll a bhailíonn,
a bheith beo.

Early-morning surge,
it will never fully ebb;
the residues that purge,
alive on this earth.

In 'Tionlacan' / 'Accompaniment', a tin mug acts a metronome for the pilgrims' journey: 'ann as, ann as, ann as, / ag imeacht as radharc'; 'tip-taps, tip-taps, tip-taps, / out of sight'. Full rhyme employed in the poem 'Oilithrigh' ('Pilgrims') – 'ceann' / 'teann; 'féin' / 'héin' – serves a similar rhythmic purpose.

In the final poem, 'Áthas' ('Joy'), the literary ego is foresworn and nothing exists beyond the moment:

Rófhada a bhíos i ngreim
ag déantús an dáin,
is go bhfuil m'aird iomlán
anois ar charn castán
á choscairt faoim chaol,
lá seo an áthais tráth an fhómhair im shaol.

Far too long I was caught up
in the craft of the poem,
while now my full attention
is on a heap of Spanish chestnuts
grinding under my heel
this joyful autumn day in life's wheel.

Bogomil Gjuzel

TO MY EX-YUGOSLAV FRIENDS FROM FYROM

How will we meet again, my friends?
Will we recognize ourselves, how
we are what we always were?

It startles me, for example, to see your faces
in the newspapers and journals
that are still available here, with articles

about or by you. How much older
you've become in these years, how
changed by all the meanwhile, mostly war.

Each of us knows it in a different way.
Hiding in a cellar, exposed to some internal
opposition. Only time accelerates in space,

fragmenting all our borders. We
are bastards in the quarrel's wake
among our European stepfathers

in world capitals, as our forefathers
were: coteries of tribe, nation, state ...
We speak our monologues to God

or to the grave. God, how my own face,
grown old, pulls the broken bits together
like a magnet. You can't see me,

perhaps – perhaps you never will.
We have eternity to catch up
with each other and our work.

We'll face each other on the Judgment Day
and pluck our eyes in disbelief,
drinking at the club named Who Was Right?

– translation of 'НА БИВШИТЕ ЈУГОСЛОВЕНСКИ ПРИЈАТЕЛИ ОД ПЈРМ-ОВЕЦ'
by **Peter H Liotta**

Note: FYROM is an acronym for the 'Former Yugoslav Republic of Macedonia'

FEATURED POET: TOBY BUCKLEY

Toby Buckley was born in Donegal. He recently finished his MA at the Seamus Heaney Centre in Belfast, and studied there as the first recipient of the Ruth West Poetry Scholarship. His work is a presence in journals and on social media. He was chosen, with twelve other poets, to participate in the Poetry Ireland Introductions readings in 2018. He also co-ordinated the important Poetry with Pride series in Belfast, which puts forward new and established voices in the LGBT+ community there. He was nominated for the GALAS Art & Literature Award last year for his work in LGBTQIA+ arts.

He is also the editor of *Bombinate*, which is described as 'a zine for new writing and ideas'. In a 2017 interview he said: "Submitting to journals and zines can be very intimidating, and my main goal with this is to make something that people feel comfortable sending their work to even if they've never really looked into publishing before."

His poems have a wide register of tone and the two published here illustrate his range of themes as well. His deft, intriguing poem 'Tree Forms as a Mother and Child' is one example. It exerts a sculptural pressure on the alloy of its subject: motherhood, trees, exploitation. The poem opens with an O'Hara like brio, sliding from disjunction into contradiction: a poem in the shape of an actual tree on the page that is hiding another meaning inside its shapes and statements. But O'Hara tends to be a jaunty and subversive user of tone. This is different.

The poem's blend of images and issues, its deliberately intrusive shape on the page as a tree – these apparently ludic pieces of style darken and sweeten into the poignance of the transformations involved. The tree will be put to use, will become a chair, a table, a birdfeeder. From the wit of these tree-shaped propositions emerges the complex under-narrative of mother and child. The poem ends up as a considerable and ambitious blend of art, wit, and argument.

The second poem, 'entryway', takes a different path, but with a similar stride. It shows irony being used to darken a poem that engages themes of the body, of sexual difference, of estrangement from the physicality of life. Following its title it juxtaposes entrances to the body that are sexual or just random, like a moth's entry into an ear. Finally, the poem, with its theme of the body's powerlessness, is a composed, small melody of disappointment and loneliness.

Toby Buckley's approach is robust and inventive. He has a command of tone and is a deft linguist. But his work opens a window into something more. I've seen, in some of the poems that come to *PIR*, a way in which younger poets are not just inventing the poem but inventing a new way to be a poet. Toby Buckley, with his communal energy, his democratic zine, and his accomplished poems, is doing just that.

– Eavan Boland

Toby Buckley

TREE FORMS AS A MOTHER AND CHILD
after Henry Moore

She's taller than physics
allows, ten times the height water
should climb before beginning to boil.
This doesn't bother her. If her pores were larger
she wouldn't be able to bring that water to her very top.
If she allowed a single bubble of air inside, all of her immaculate
tubing would be killed. She's the poster girl for intelligent design.
Her freshest parts raise clear and high above the ground:
birds' nests, beehives, cocoons, baby squirrels, frisbees, secret huts.
She is stronger than any one of us. The children often forget her
thick skin doesn't mean she isn't alive and vibrant, doesn't mean
she doesn't feel every word carved into the surface of her.
She brings us shade, shelter and fresh air
then lets us whittle her into something
more useful –
a chair
a table
a card
a model
of a tree
a beebox
a birdfeeder.

Toby Buckley

ENTRYWAY

i have had bad experiences
of things
going inside of things

sometimes words
slipping into my open ears
or boy things going inside
like wrong jigsaw pieces
leaving the smaller piece
sad and dogeared

one time a moth
crawled into my
ear in the middle
of the night

i had to spend six
hours in a&e
and when the doctor tried
to pull it out he cut open my
ear canal

and i couldn't go in
the sea for two
to three weeks

Hugh O'Donnell

TIME OUT

The sax wanders in and carries me off
to New Orleans or to a poky restaurant
in Montmartre where a waiter approaches
whom I dismiss, my eye suddenly taken
by the hands outside Bowe's pub stuck
at five to six to mark a seismic shudder,
head-butt, or a long drawn-out falling out
as a woman with a book squeezes in …
A new track opens up with Odetta singing
Dylan in a bluesy voice, 'Don't think twice,
it's alright' while monsieur sips Earl Grey
tea, counting all the dead musicians since
1962. "O," she says up close, "Don't you
like Django?" "Sorry," I stall. "Yes, I do. I do."

Books Upstairs, D'Olier Street 1978-2018

Janet Shepperson

ALL THE BOOKS IN THE UNIVERSE

All the books in the universe have been swallowed
by a bulbous, shadowy whale called *cyberspace.*
His tiny single eye glows all night long.
Paddle your fingers on his shiny skin
and words (not always the right ones) tumble out
of his shifty mouth in glistening chunks of spittle,
skewing your eyes like the glare on a tilting wave.

Think of a crow without feathers. A fox without fur.
A garden with no leaves. A house with no books.
He's crunched their spines and pulverized their covers:
no Moll, no Chatterley, no Bovary,
no Dalloway or Copperfield or Tess.
Nothing to burrow into or hide behind.
Bare walls, devoid of bookshelves, shivering.

He has shrunk the world to a flat, sleek rectangle.
No subtle heady smell of printer's glue,
soft *crump* of flicking pages. Nothing to fold.
You sit like Victorian children with tight little slates,
awaiting instructions. Answer inscribe rub out.
No doodling annotating scribbling in margins –
no offcuts of your life preserved as bookmarks –

no cinema tickets, letters, leaves, pressed flowers –
what kind of a machine eats leaves and flowers?
There's just this black thing gulping its daily dose
from a trio of holes in the wall. If the well runs dry,
there'll be no mottled stains unravelling,
no last gasps. Just a sudden snap into blankness.
No echoes fading out. No ghosts of words.

Tristram Fane Saunders

RUN OF THE MILL

> *The bounded is loathed by its possessor; the same dull round, even*
> *of a universe, would soon become a mill with complicated wheels.*
>   – William Blake

By current estimates, I've spanned
a quarter of a life
oiling the gears' teeth, drawing plans,
tinkering with love,

and now at length the work is done.
The mill is running well
and grinding smooth. This little hell
is vast and dim.

There is no millstone, belt or band
with angles wide enough
to crack the chaff below it, and
the air above.

Trapped by the skin outside my skin,
this wheel for bone and shell,
I'll do the one thing I do well
and burrow *in*.

Manus Charleton

RICHARD MURPHY AT EIGHTY
        In Sligo for the Yeats summer school, 2007

It had to be him, we thought,
Richard Murphy the poet
Out for a late evening stroll
Along the boardwalk of the Glasshouse Hotel
By the edge of the Garavogue.
Beside him a companion
And while they went by the bench where we sat
The patter of their conversation
Mingled with the river's constant proclamation
Of whatever is, will pass.

I had been saying how I felt dispirited
And on seeing him, a veteran Bohemian
Still about on a walking-stick
And carrying a satchel over his shoulder,
The mood lifted.
A poet-sailor, you said, and I saw him
Still drawn to the beguiling sea
For its sway and slap against the bow,
Still sailing his Galway hooker
From Cleggan to High Island,
Still prepared to flounder
Among Atlantic crests and troughs
To catch a trace of the Muse's maddening voice
From the ceaseless flux.

Steven Jay Bourke

WHERE IS THE BALL?

Among the long grasses,

by the bramble wall,

where runs a path along which
a wraith or a wrankle might slip

in the drift, slowly, only to recur:

The hearing of deeds to which we are deaf and
the seeing of things to which we are blind.[1]

---

1 Plutarch, *Morals* (100 CE; translated into English by Philemon Holland, 1603 CE), writing on memory, or, as Plutarch phrased it, 'divination in reverse', paraphrasing the self-description of the Pythian oracle, namely: 'the deaf man's hearing, and the blind man's sight', as imparted to the Aeolians of Thessaly, while inquiring about the expulsion of the Boeotians at Arnê.

Sally Van Doren

DOUBLE ENTENDRE

I'd really like to reveal
myself to you, but I am
prevented from doing so
by my frenum, the muscle
between my two front teeth
that acts as a body guard
whenever I turn my sights
inward to dispel the lethargy
swarming around the analyst
in me who doesn't want to look
under my tongue. Would
you either? I'm finally alone
in my quiet mouth. Let's make
a pact. If I don't unearth
my weaknesses, then I won't
bury you with them. I'll spend
all night gargling with warm
salt water to practice. Then,
in the morning, we'll put our
fingers down our throats
and see who wins.

Notes on Contributors

Gary Allen has published sixteen books of poetry, most recently *Bridges* (Dempsey and Windle, 2017). A new collection, *The Glass King*, is just published by Stairwell Books. He has published widely in magazines, including *Australian Book Review*, *The London Magazine*, *New Statesman*, *The Poetry Review*, and *The Threepenny Review*.

Dermot J Archer is a former lecturer in Literature and Creative Writing for Queen's University, Belfast. He has poems either published or forthcoming in *Stand*, *Orbis*, *Envoi*, *THE SHOp*, *Cyphers*, *Parnassus*, *Penwood Review*, *Quiddity International Literary Journal* (Illinois Public Radio), *The Café Review*, and *The Old Red Rimono*.

Mark Baker won the Listowel Writer's Week Poetry Collection prize in 2015. He has been published in a variety of journals and magazines. He was selected for the Poetry Ireland Introductions readings in 2009.

John Wall Barger's poems appear in *The American Poetry Review*, *Rattle*, *The Cincinnati Review*, and *Best of the Best Canadian Poetry*. His poem 'Smog Mother' was a co-winner of *The Malahat Review*'s 2017 Long Poem Prize. He lives in Philadelphia, and is on the editorial board of *Painted Bride Quarterly*.

Partridge Boswell is the author of *Some Far Country* (Grolier Poetry Press), winner of the Grolier Prize in 2013. His poems have recently appeared in *Gettysburg Review*, *Salmagundi*, *The American Poetry Review*, and *Plume*. He co-founded Bookstock literary festival and the poetry / music group Los Lorcas. He teaches at Burlington Writers Workshop, and lives with his family in Vermont.

Steven Jay Bourke is an Irish poet, now living in Ethiopia. A graduate of Columbia University, he is completing a first collection, *Feet*.

Toby Buckley – see page 125.

David Butler's second poetry collection, *All the Barbaric Glass*, was published in 2017 by Doire Press. In the same year, he completed a Per Cent poetry commission entitled *Blackrock Sequence*. His awards for poetry include the Féile Filíochta, Ted McNulty, Brendan Kennelly, Phizzfest, Baileborough, and Poetry Ireland / Trócaire prizes.

Mairéad Byrne is Professor of Poetry + Poetics at Rhode Island School of Design, teaching courses in Sound Poetry, Visual Poetry, Digital Poetics, Material Poetics, Contemporary Poetry, and poetry workshops. She has published six collections, most recently *Famosa na sua cabeça* (Dobra Editorial, 2015), and runs *couscous*, a performance series of diverse poetries.

Moya Cannon's most recent collection of poems is *Keats Lives* (Carcanet Press, 2015). She was born in Co Donegal and lives in Dublin. She has edited *Poetry Ireland Review*, and was the 2011 Heimbold Chair of Irish Studies at Villanova University.

Eleni Cay is a Slovakian-born poet living in the UK. Her most recent poems were published by Eyewear Publishing in 2017, and appeared in *Atticus Review, Glasgow Review of Books, Acumen,* and *Envoi*. Eleni's award-winning collection of Slovak poems, *A Butterfly's Trembling in the Digital Age,* was translated by John Minahane and published by Parthian Books. Eleni is known for her filmpoems, dancepoems, and multimedia poetry, which have been screened at international festivals and featured on *Button Poetry*. See www.eleni-cay.com.

Manus Charleton's essays have appeared regularly in *The Dublin Review of Books*. He has also had essays and short fiction published in *Irish Pages*, including two essays on Seamus Heaney, 'Ethical Depth' and 'Heaney and the Moderns'. 'Richard Murphy at Eighty' in this issue is his first published poem. See www.manuscharleton.ie

Lucy Collins is Associate Professor of English at University College Dublin. Her most recent book is *Contemporary Irish Women Poets: Memory and Estrangement* (Liverpool University Press, 2015). She is co-founder of the Irish Poetry Reading Archive, a national digital repository.

Ben Dombroski is a poet and teacher living in Savannah, Georgia. In addition to *Best New Poets* (2009), his work has appeared in *Gettysburg Review, Spillway, Hunger Mountain,* and elsewhere.

Sally Van Doren, a poet and artist, is the author of three collections from LSU Press: *Promise* (2017), *Possessive* (2012), and *Sex at Noon Taxes* (2008), which received the Walt Whitman Award from the Academy of American Poets. She posts daily lines from her ongoing poem, *The Sense Series,* via Instagram @sallyvandoren.

Martina Evans grew up in Co Cork and trained in Dublin as a radiographer, before moving to London in 1988. She is the author of eleven books of poetry and prose. *Now We Can Talk Openly About Men* was published earlier this year by Carcanet Press.

Attracta Fahy, from Co Galway, a mother and psychotherapist, completed her MA in writing at NUIG in 2017. She participates in the Over The Edge poetry workshops. Her poems have been published in *Banshee*, *The Blue Nib*, *The Lake*, *Burning House Press*, *Crossways Literary Magazine*, *North West Words*, *Dodging the Rain*, *Coast to Coast to Coast*, and *The Galway Review*.

Peter Fallon's recent books are *Strong, My Love* and *Deeds and Their Days* (after Hesiod). He is founder (1970-), editor, and publisher of The Gallery Press. A member of the Hinterland house band, he lives in Loughcrew in Co Meath where he farmed for many years.

James Finnegan, born in Dublin, was highly commended in the Patrick Kavanagh Poetry Competition, and has published work in *The Irish Times*, *HNIW*, *Cyphers*, *Skylight47*, *North West Words*, and the anthology *Best New British & Irish Poets 2018* (Eyewear Publishing). He holds a Ph.D in living educational theory. His first full collection of poems, *Half-Open Door*, is just published by Eyewear Publishing.

Amy Gaffney is from Kildare. She is co-editor in chief of *HCE Review Literary Journal* 2017-2018, and will graduate with an MA in Creative Writing from UCD in December 2018. She mainly writes fiction, but intends to continue writing poetry surrounding issues of identity for Irish women and mothers.

Owen Gallagher was born of Irish parents in the Gorbals area of Glasgow. He lives in London. His previous publications are *Sat Guru Snowman* (Peterloo Poets, 2001), *Tea with the Taliban* (Smokestack Books, 2012), and *A Good Enough Love* (Salmon Poetry, 2015).

Peggie Gallagher's work has appeared in literary journals in Ireland, England, and North America. She was shortlisted for the Strokestown International and Gregory O'Donoghue poetry awards, and won the Listowel Writer's Week Poetry Collection prize in 2012. Her first collection, *Tilth*, is published by Arlen House.

Matthew Geden was born and brought up in the English Midlands. He moved to Kinsale in 1990. His most recent poetry collection is *The Place Inside* (Dedalus Press, 2012). He is the Director of Kinsale Writing School.

Ray Givans has been published in five pamphlet-length poetry collections – the most recent is *The Innermost Room* (Poetry Salzburg Press, 2017). His first full collection, *Tolstoy in Love*, was published by Dedalus Press in 2009 and was shortlisted for the Strong award.

Bogomil Gjuzel is a Macedonian poet, prose writer, playwright, and translator. Considered by Charles Simic to be 'Macedonia's greatest living poet', Gjuzel was born in 1939 in Čačak, Serbia. Winner of many awards and fellowships, he was one of the ten founders of the Association of Independent Writers of Macedonia, and he served as acting director of the Struga Poetry Evenings International Festival from 1999-2003. *Surviving: Selected Poems 1962-2012* is available in an English / Macedonian edition (Blesok Publishing, 2012). He lives in Skopje.

Mark Granier lives in Bray, Co Wicklow. His awards include The Vincent Buckley Poetry Prize and two Patrick and Katherine Kavanagh Fellowships. His fifth collection, *Ghostlight: New & Selected Poems*, was published by Salmon Poetry in May 2017.

Kerry Hardie's most recent collection is *The Zebra Stood in The Night*, (Bloodaxe Books, 2014). She has published six previous collections as well as a Selected Poems, and another collection is forthcoming. She has also written a radio play, two novels, and has recently completed a third.

Lynn Harding is an editor from Cork, living and working in Dublin. Her poetry has been published in *The Irish Times*, featured on Dublin South FM's *Rhyme and Reason* radio arts programme, and performed across Ireland and Northern Ireland.

James Harpur's latest book is *The White Silhouette* (Carcanet Press, 2018), which includes meditations on *The Book of Kells*, Rublev's icons, and pilgrimage. He lives in West Cork.

Fred Johnston was born in Belfast and educated both there and in Toronto. A poet, short story writer, and novelist, he has reviewed for *Harpers & Queen, The Irish Times, The Southern Review, Books Ireland, The Sunday Times*, and for RTÉ. A new collection of poems, *Rogue States*, is due out later this year from Salmon Poetry. He received a Prix de l'Ambassade for work on translations in 2002, and in 2004 he was writer-in-residence to the Princess Grace Irish Library at Monaco. He lives in Galway.

EE Jones is a writer, activist, and community campaigner living in Oxfordshire, England. She studied Modern History and English at the University of Oxford, and her poems have appeared in *Acumen* and *The Journal*, with further publication forthcoming in *Stand*. Her poem 'For An Unknown Migrant' was long-listed for the UK's National Poetry Competition (2016).

Patrick Kehoe's two collections of poetry are *Its Words You Want* (Salmon Poetry, 2011), and *The Cask of Moonlight* (Dedalus Press, 2014.) A new volume, *Places to Sleep*, was published by Salmon Poetry in June this year. He was born in Enniscorthy, Co Wexford, where he currently lives.

Shannon Kelly's writing and translation has appeared in *Crannóg, The Irish Times*, and *BODY Prague*. She was the 2016 winner of the Allingham Festival Poetry Competition, and was selected as one of the 50 best new British and Irish poets of 2018 by Eyewear Publishing. She lives in Galway.

John Kinsella's most recent books of poetry include *Drowning in Wheat: Selected Poems* (Picador Poetry, 2017) and *The Wound* (Arc, 2018). He is Professor of Literature and Environment at Curtin University, Western Australia, and a Fellow of Churchill College, Cambridge.

David Knowles moved to Donegal in 2014 to study Irish. He worked closely with Cathal Ó Searcaigh on both the poet's work and the beautiful Cloich Chionnaola dialect.

Julie Hungiville LeMay is the author of the poetry collection, *The Echo of Ice Letting Go* (University of Alaska Press, 2017). She holds an MFA in Creative Writing from Antioch University, Los Angeles, where she served as poetry editor for Antioch's literary journal, *Lunch Ticket*. She lives in Alaska's Matanuska Valley.

Peter H Liotta (1957-2012) was Professor of Political Science and Humanities at Salve Regina University, and Executive Director of the Pell Centre for International Relations and Public Policy. A published writer of poetry and prose, he also translated the work of Macedonian poet Bogomil Gjuzel.

Ailbhe McDaid is a Ph.D graduate of the Centre for Irish and Scottish Studies at the University of Otago, New Zealand. She is an incoming Irish Research Council Postdoctoral Research Fellow at UCC, and author of *The Poetics of Migration in Contemporary Irish Poetry* (Palgrave Macmillan, 2017).

Sean H McDowell teaches at Seattle University. He edits the *John Donne Journal* and has published many essays on Renaissance and contemporary Irish poets. His poems have appeared in *Clover, The Best of Vine Leaves Literary Journal, Scintilla,* and *The Lyric,* and work is also forthcoming in *The High Window.*

Kiera McGarry was born in Co Antrim, and studied at the Seamus Heaney centre for Poetry, graduating in 2016. Her work, which often considers subjects from the natural world and rural life, has appeared in journals and anthologies, including *the future always makes me so thirsty: New Poets from the North of Ireland* (Blackstaff Press, 2016).

Scott McKendry's poems have appeared in *The Tangerine, Public Illumination Magazine, The Manchester Review, Magma,* and *Cyphers.* His work was anthologised in *the future always makes me so thirsty: New Poets from the North of Ireland* (Blackstaff Press, 2016).

Ethna McKiernan has been twice awarded a Minnesota State Arts Board grant in poetry. Her first book was a Minnesota Book Award Nominee, and her second and third books were published by Salmon Poetry. She works for a non-profit organisation serving the Minneapolis homeless population.

Derek Mahon's *New Collected Poems* appeared in 2011. 'Ophelia' and 'Trump Time' appear in *Against the Clock* which is published by The Gallery Press in August 2018.

Martin Malone lives in Scotland. He has published two poetry collections: *The Waiting Hillside* (Templar Poetry, 2011) and *Cur* (Shoestring, 2015). His Great War-related third collection, *The Unreturning,* is forthcoming. He is an associate teaching fellow in creative writing at Aberdeen University, has recently completed a Ph.D in poetry at Sheffield University, and he edits *The Interpreter's House* poetry journal.

Oliver Mort is from Belfast. He holds a Ph.D in American Literature. His poetry has been published in *The Rialto, The Yellow Nib,* and elsewhere. He has new work due to appear in *Wasafiri* and *Boyne Berries,* later in 2018.

Jade Murphy, born in Galway, is a fourth year student of the BA with Creative Writing at the NUI Galway, under the mentorship of Mike McCormack and Elaine Feeney. She is currently working towards her first chapbook, *In a London Fish Shop.*

Hugh O'Donnell's collection, *No Place Like It*, was published by Doghouse Books. His book of reflections on the natural world, *Songs for the Slow Lane*, appeared in 2014 from Columba Press. Recently, he had work in *Migrant Shores: Irish, Moroccan & Galician Poetry*, edited by Manuela Palacios (Salmon Poetry, 2017).

Proinsias Ó Drisceoil is the author of many books and essays on the Gaelic literature of Ireland and Scotland. He has judged the Oireachtas Poetry Awards on a number of occasions. He has a particular interest in poetry in Scottish Gaelic and in literary production from the south east of Ireland.

Nessa O'Mahony is a Dublin-born poet. She has published four books of poetry – *Bar Talk* (Italics Press, 1999), *Trapping a Ghost* (bluechrome publishing, 2005), *In Sight of Home* (Salmon Poetry, 2009), and *Her Father's Daughter* (Salmon Poetry, 2014). With Paul Munden she co-edited *Metamorphic: 21st century poets respond to Ovid* (Recent Work Press, 2017).

Liam Ó Muirthile (1950-2018): his *An Fuíoll Feá: Rogha Dánta / Woodcuttings: New and Selected Poems* was published by Cois Life in 2013.

Kate O'Neill's poetry appears in the *Taos Journal of the Arts* and the *Journal of War, Literature and the Arts*, among other outlets. She is a 2018 Fellow at Vermont Studio Centre, teaches at the University of New Mexico, and holds an MFA from the Institute of American Indian Arts and an Ed.D from Harvard.

Liam O'Neill, originally from Kilkenny, lives in Galway where he works with people with disabilities. He is a prize-winner in the Strokestown 20/20 competition, and has been shortlisted for the Hennessy Prize 2018. He has a non-fiction ebook available on Amazon, entitled *All the Days of Winter*.

Linda Opyr, the Nassau County Poet Laureate 2011-13, is the author of seven collections of poetry. Her poems have appeared in anthologies, journals, magazines, and newspapers, including *The Hudson Review*, *The Atlanta Review*, *The Paterson Literary Review*, *Crannóg*, and *The New York Times*. She lives on Long Island, NY.

Frank Ormsby has published six collections of poems, most recently *Goat's Milk: New and Selected Poems* (Bloodaxe Books, 2015) and *The Darkness of Snow* (Bloodaxe Books, 2017). As editor of *The Honest Ulsterman* magazine for twenty years, and as editor of *Poets from the North of Ireland* and *A Rage for Order: Poetry of the Northern Ireland Troubles*, he was a central figure in the burgeoning of Ulster poetry since the 1960s. He is currently editor, with Leontia Flynn, of the poetry magazine *The Yellow Nib*.

Cathal Ó Searcaigh's *The View from the Glen: Selected Prose* was published earlier this year by The Onslaught Press.

Art Ó Súilleabháin has published a number of books of poetry *as Gaeilge* for children. He is currently working on a collection of poetry in English. He lives in Corr na Móna in Co Galway.

Jane Robinson is the author of *Journey to the Sleeping Whale* (Salmon Poetry, 2018). She won the Strokestown International Poetry Prize and the Red Line Poetry Competition, and was joint runner-up for the Patrick Kavanagh Award. She has a Ph.D in science from the California Institute of Technology, and she lives in Dublin.

Gabriel Rosenstock, poet, tankaist, haikuist, essayist, playwright, and novelist, was born in 1949 in postcolonial Ireland. His Irish-language versions of Goan poetry appeared recently in the bilingual anthology *Goa: A Garland of Poems* (The Onslaught Press, 2017). He blogs at http://roghaghabriel.blogspot.ie/

Julie-Ann Rowell's pamphlet *Convergence* (Brodie Press, 2003) won a PBS Award. Her collection *Letters North* (Brodie Press, 2008) was nominated for the Michael Murphy Poetry Prize for Best First Collection in Britain and Ireland, in 2011. Her latest collection, *Voices in the Garden* (2015), about Joan of Arc, is published by Lapwing Publications, Belfast.

Robyn Rowland has published 10 poetry books, most recently *Mosaics from the Map* (Doire Press, 2018) and *This Intimate War: Gallipoli/Çanakkale 1915 – İçli Dışlı Bir Savaş: Gelibolu/Çanakkale 1915*, with Turkish translations by Mehmet Ali Çelikel (Five Islands, 2015; Spinifex, 2018). Her work is online at the Irish Poetry Reading Archive in UCD.

Tristram Fane Saunders lives in London. His poems have been published in journals including *The London Magazine* and *The Dark Horse*. His most recent pamphlet, *Postcards from Sulpicia* (Tapsalteerie, 2015), is a translation of Ancient Rome's only extant female poet, Sulpicia.

John W Sexton's sixth poetry collection, *Futures Pass*, has recently been published by Salmon Poetry. His poem 'The Green Owl' was awarded the Listowel Poetry Prize in 2007 for best single poem, and in that same year he was awarded a Patrick and Katherine Kavanagh Fellowship.

Katie Sheehan is originally from Chicago and currently lives in Dublin. Her poetry has previously appeared in magazines such as *Contemporary Verse 2*, *The Moth*, and *Southword*, and she read for the 2013 Poetry Ireland Introductions readings.

Janet Shepperson was born in Edinburgh and has lived in Belfast since 1977. She has published poetry widely in periodicals, pamphlets, and in two full collections: *The Aphrodite Stone* (Salmon Poetry, 1995) and *Eve Complains to God* (Lagan Press, 2004). Her debut novel, *Vinny's Wilderness*, was published by Liberties Press in 2016.

Peter Sirr has published ten collections with The Gallery Press, most recently *Sway* (2016), versions of poems from the troubadour tradition. *The Rooms* (2014) was shortlisted for *The Irish Times* Poetry Now Award and the Pigott Poetry Prize. *The Thing Is* (2009) was awarded the Michael Hartnett Prize in 2011. He lives in Dublin and is a member of Aosdána.

Knute Skinner's collected poems, *Fifty Years: Poems 1957-2007*, was published by Salmon Poetry in 2007. A limited edition of his poems, translated into Italian by Roberto Nassi, appeared from Damocle Edizioni, Chioggia, Italy. His most recent collections are *Concerned Attentions*, (Salmon Poetry, 2013), *Against All Odds* (Lapwing Publications, 2016), and *The Life That I Have* (Salmon Poetry, 2018).

Arun Sood was born and raised in Scotland, to a Gaelic-speaking West-Highland mother and a Hindi-speaking Indian father who emigrated to Glasgow in the 1970s. He writes essays, articles, and poems that focus on cultural memory and the intersections between self, history, and landscape.

Dawn Sullivan, originally from London, now spends most of her time writing and painting in Co Kerry, and has been published in *Poetry Ireland Review* and *Aquarius*. She participated in the Poetry Ireland Introductions readings in 2003.

Rosamund Taylor won the Mairtín Crawford Award in 2017. She has been nominated for a Forward Prize, and was twice short-listed for the Montreal International Poetry Prize. Her work is widely published in the UK and Ireland, and appears in *The Best New British and Irish Poets* anthology (Eyewear Publishing, 2018).

Iain Twiddy lived for several years in northern Japan. His poetry has been accepted by a number of publications, including *The Honest Ulsterman* and *The London Magazine*.

Laura Paul Watson lives and writes in Pine, Colorado. She is a graduate of the MFA program at the University of Florida. Her work has also appeared in *The Massachusetts Review*, *Conduit*, and *Poetry Northwest*, among other publications.

Joyce Wilson edits *The Poetry Porch* (www.poetryporch.com), an online magazine. Her poetry collection *The Etymology of Spruce* (Rock Village Publishing), and a chapbook *The Springhouse* (Finishing Line Press), both appeared in 2010. Her poems have appeared in many literary journals, including *Alabama Literary Review* and *American Arts Quarterly*.